Tea with the Angel Lady

To Dorothy and George —
Blessings
Marilynn + Bill Webber

Tea with the Angel Lady

Heartwarming Stories and Programs for Teas with a Complete Guide to Preparing Tea for One or One Hundred

By Marilynn Carlson Webber
with William Webber

xulon
PRESS

The author, Marilynn, enjoying tea at age five.

Tea with the Angel Lady
by Marilynn Carlson Webber with Bill Webber

Printed in the United States of America
ISBN 1-931232-65-2

Xulon Press
11350 Random Hills Road
Suite 800
Fairfax, VA 22030
(703) 279-6511
XulonPress.com

Dedication

To my granddaughters,
Aubrey and Angela Webber. and Linnea Scott,
who share my passion for tea

Contents

The Angel Lady

Chapter One

From Cathedral to Casino

By Bill Webber, husband of the Angel Lady

One of the questions I am asked most frequently is this, "Why is your wife called the Angel Lady?"

It all began when Marilynn was four years old. As a child growing up in Chicago bedtime was difficult for her, and she was afraid of the dark. Mother Carlson tried everything to help her. She would tell bedtime stories and sing songs to her, but always Marilynn would plead with her to stay in her room, at least until she was sound asleep. One night after Marilynn was tucked into bed her mother said, "Marilynn, I have a surprise for you." First Mother Carlson read from the ninety-first Psalm, "For he shall give his angels charge over thee, to keep thee in all thy ways"(v.11). Next she explained that God had appointed a special angel, just for her, to be her guardian angel. Even while she slept, her mother explained, the guardian angel kept watch over her. Although she couldn't see him, he was always with her. Then Mother Carlson reached into a bag and took out an angel figurine. It was made of plaster, its robe was painted a soft pink, and it was about five inches tall. When she placed it on the dresser Marilynn thought it was the most beautiful thing she had ever seen. *I will always keep it,* she promised to herself. Comforted by the thought of a guardian angel protecting her, the little girl fell asleep.

The next day the little Marilynn began her angel collection. She would save her birthday money, go to the five and ten cent store, and ask, "Please show me your angels."

The clerk would look at her with some amusement and say, "Little girl, angels are just for Christmas."

"O no they are not!" Marilynn would insist. "Angels are always with us. My angel is with me right now."

The clerk would smile patronizingly at her and tell her to come back when the Christmas ornaments were on sale. Through the years her angel collection grew, but very slowly.

A Life Changing Encounter

When Marilynn was fourteen, her parents moved from Chicago to suburban Wheaton, Illinois. Since there were only a few weeks left of the school term, Marilynn stayed in Chicago with a friend and completed her freshman year at Austin High School. On the weekends she took the train to her new home in Wheaton. One Friday, just before she boarded the Chicago and Northwestern train for the trip home, she learned that her favorite Sunday School teacher had a terminal illness and had just a short time to live. This was Marilynn's first experience with death coming to someone close to her and it was difficult for her to accept. Although she tried to comfort herself with thoughts of heaven, she could not understand why bad things happen to good people. As she made the thirty-nine-mile trip to her new home her sadness grew more profound.

By habit she got off the westbound train at the College

Avenue Station. By this time she was so depressed she was unaware of her surroundings. She began to cross the three sets of tracks to make her way home when suddenly she was brought out of her reverie by the frightening blast of a train whistle. She was on the tracks and the approaching locomotive was so close she could see the blue eyes and terrified face of the engineer. But Marilynn was frozen with fear. She could not move. *I'm going to die,* she thought. *I'll be in heaven before my Sunday School teacher.*

An instant before the train would have hit her Marilynn was pushed as if a giant had shoved her from behind. She went flying off the tracks, down the siding, scraping her knees on the cinders. She scrambled to her feet, grateful to be alive, and wondering who the hero was who had pushed her and saved her life. No one was there! The tracks were elevated and she could see for blocks. There was not a person in sight. In that moment Marilynn knew that her life had been saved by her guardian angel. She rushed home and told her mother. After all, it was her mother who had taught her about guardian angels! But Marilynn did not tell her teenage friends because she was certain that they would think she was weird.

In the years that followed Marilynn began studying what the Bible had to say about the heavenly hosts and she became a serious angel collector. Twenty years ago when Billy Graham's book *Angels, God's Secret Agents,* was published people became more interested in the subject Marilynn had loved all her life. Friends who knew she collected angels began to ask Marilynn to come to their group, display some of her collection, and talk on angels. *Guideposts* magazine decided to do an entire issue on angels, and the editor asked her to write the lead article. When it came out Evelyn Jacobson, the president of the Angel Collectors Club of America, called on the telephone and said, "Since you are so interested in angels, you must join our organization." Marilynn was delighted to learn she was not the only serious collector and joined the group eagerly. In 1987 they invited Marilynn to be the keynote speaker for the Angel Collectors Club of America convention in Golden, Colorado.

Marilynn's Angel Store

At that time it was a challenge to find new angels for her collection. When Marilynn complained that the stores did not have any angels, I would tell my wife, "Someone must be making angels. You need to get your license and go to the wholesale marts and gift shows and find the companies who have angels to offer."

She did. In 1989 Marilynn began the first all angel store. Today there are many all angel stores and angel merchandise can be found everywhere, but at that time there were few angels to be found anywhere. At the gift shows the wholesale dealers would say, "Lady, angels are just for Christmas. Come back for the Christmas show and you can buy angel ornaments then."

"Angels are not just for Christmas," Marilynn insisted. "There is a growing interest in angels. You need to begin to add them to your line or you will lose out on the coming market." She later learned that many of the sales reps took the word back to their companies, and her message was seriously discussed in board rooms from Los Angeles to New York. Now when the vendors see her they call out, "Angel Lady, come and see the new angels we have made." What a wonderful change!

The Explosion of Interest in Angels

Joan Wester Anderson, Eileen Freeman, and Marilynn were talking over lunch at the Angels of the World International convention in 1992 about the explosion of interest in angels. They agreed to take the opportunities that would come their way to spread the word about the heavenly hosts. The opportunities were not long in coming. One morning Marilynn answered the telephone and was startled to hear David Briggs from the Associated Press say, "Marilynn, I understand you are one of the five experts on angels in the United States."

"I am?" she gasped. She had loved angels since childhood and had studied everything she could find about them, but she never considered herself to be an expert. Following the interview, the Associated Press told Marilynn's story in hundreds of papers across the country. In the months that followed she was interviewed by *TIME* magazine, *The Ladies Home Journal*, the major television networks, radio stations, and newspapers. Marilynn became a popular guest on television and radio talk shows.

Guideposts magazine carried an article Marilynn had written about a woman who had had an experience with an angel. After the article appeared, letters began to come in the mail. At first there were ten to twenty each day. After a week she began to receive over two hundred letters a day. The mailman noticed. There were far to many for him to stuff into our mailbox so he would have to ring our doorbell. One day, somewhat exasperated, he asked, "Mrs. Webber, what in the world is going on here? Are you selling drugs by mail or something?"

"Oh, no," Marilynn replied. "These letters are from people who have read an article I wrote for a magazine. Would you like to read it?"

"I guess so," the mailman answered without enthusiasm. Marilynn gave him a copy of the magazine. The next day the postman returned with his arms filled with hundreds more letters.

"Did you read the article?" Marilynn asked.

"Yes," the mailman replied, "and it helped me make a

decision."

Marilynn was burning with curiosity. "What decision did you make?" she inquired.

"The post office has offered me an early retirement, and I am going to take it!" the letter carrier asserted. He did take the early retirement, and we lost the best mailman we had ever had.

When it was over Marilynn had received over 8,500 letters in response to that one article. This was especially exciting because many people were writing to share their own angel story.

A Rustle of Angels

Drawing on this marvelous resource as well as the accounts of angel encounters Marilynn had been collecting for years, she wrote a book called *A Rustle of Angels*. Marilynn contributed the true stories of angels in the lives of people today. For this book we became a husband and wife team, and I used my training in theology and added the Biblical and theological insights, written in an easy to read *Reader's Digest* style. Published in 1994, *A Rustle of Angels* filled a need for a book coming from a mainstream Christian perspective. The book sold over a quarter million copies in its first year and won the print media award from the Excellence in Media Foundation. To our joy the award they presented us was a statue of an angel. Now the book has sold over 300,000 copies in English in hardback and has appeared in foreign language editions.

As Marilynn wrote the book she talked to many people who had seen an angel. *How fortunate they were,* she thought. She had always wanted to see an angel. Although an angel had saved her life on the railroad tracks when she was a teen, she did not see this guardian spirit. She knew that in the Bible angels are never summoned. They come only when God sends them for his purposes.

Four Angels Dressed in Black

But they did come to Marilynn one night in a dream. There were four angels, dressed in black. Even their wings were black. They were in mourning. *These are not the glorious, beautiful angels I wanted to see,* Marilynn thought. She asked the one closest to her at the head of her bed, "Why are you so sad?"

"We are sad because you are dying," the angel replied. "Unless something is done, you are going to die."

Then they were gone. Instantly Marilynn woke, then told me the angel's message. "What do you think it means?" she probed.

"I think you need to see a doctor right away," I replied firmly.

Marilynn had not seen a doctor for years. Our family doctor had retired and had referred her to another physician. That doctor moved his practice to another state. Next Marilynn went to a woman doctor, but soon this doctor joined the army! But she referred Marilynn to the Loma Linda Clinic. When Marilynn had called, the nurse told her all the doctors were completely filled, the clinic had a two-year wait list, and they were taking no new patients. Marilynn intended to find another doctor, but since she was not feeling sick, she kept putting it off. Now four years had passed without a doctor's visit.

The next morning I called the Loma Linda Clinic. "My wife must see a doctor right away," I insisted.

"Can you tell me what is so urgent?" the nurse replied.

So I told her about the angels "Just a moment, I'm going to put you on hold," the nurse told me. A minute later she was back on the line. "The doctor will see your wife Wednesday," she said. God had taken care of the two-year waiting list.

When Marilynn saw the doctor he said, "What's this I hear about angels?" Marilynn recounted her experience with the four angels dressed in black, and the doctor wrote it at the beginning of her medical history. The doctor did a biopsy and ordered a full battery of tests. When Marilynn returned for the results the doctor said, "You have cancer and must have surgery right away. You should be thankful for the warning the angels gave you. With the kind of cancer you have there are no symptoms until it is too late."

Loma Linda is a teaching hospital, and in the next several days many doctors, residents, and interns examined her. They would look at her medical record and say, "Tell us about the angels."

Her surgery was September 2, 1993. Praise God, the surgeon was able to remove all the cancer. Marilynn has been faithful in her follow up visits, and the doctor assures her she is cancer free.

Marilynn believes the main way God gives his messages today is through the Bible, the life and teachings of Jesus Christ, and through the Holy Spirit within. But she is living proof that God still uses his angels to give messages today when it is needed.

Marilynn's Angel Teas

Marilynn fell in love with the British teatime when we spent a summer doing an exchange pastorate in England. When we returned home to the United States, Marilynn began serving tea to friends who would come to her home. Soon they began to ask if they could return with other friends, chat about angels, and enjoy afternoon tea with us. To Marilynn's surprise the Orange County Register and other newspapers wrote features about having tea with the Angel Lady. Soon we were having groups come to tea several times a week.

We served a three course tea. I would make scones and Devonshire cream and join Marilynn as we talked about God's love and care as seen in the ministry of the angels. One day I answered the telephone. To my surprise it was a television producer calling from London, England asking if they could come and film one of our teas. Caught by surprise, I replied, "You've got to be kidding. We go to England to learn about tea. The British don't come to Southern California." But come they did. They filmed Marilynn's collection of four thousand angels, how we served tea, and our conversation about angels. I was featured in the kitchen baking scones. Later the British television company sent us a copy of the video and a note that said they had good news and bad news for us. The good news was that over half of the television sets in England had been tuned in to Marilynn's angel tea. The bad news was that Bill and his scones had ended up on the cutting room.

From Cathedral to Casino

God is full of surprises! Looking back Marilynn can see that it was God who put the idea in her mother's mind to comfort her when she was a frightened four-year-old girl by teaching her about angels. But for years as Marilynn's interest in angels grew and her collection expanded, she thought this was a purely personal passion. People were surprised by the explosion of interest in angels that began about 1992, most of it New Age and outside the church, but God was not surprised. Looking back Marilynn can see that God had been preparing her since she was a child so that when the explosion of interest in angels came Marilynn could be in the center of it to give a clear witness about the Biblical teachings about angels.

In her wildest dreams Marilynn never thought she would

be the author of a best selling book on angels, a guest on hundreds of radio and television shows talking about angels, a consultant for network specials about angels, and provide material for prime time television shows in sweeps week. She has spoken to hundreds of groups and led many retreats and seminars about angels, literally from cathedrals to casinos. She was the guest speaker on Dr. Robert Schuller's global telecast from the Crystal Cathedral and spoke at their International Women's Conference. Then two weeks later she was at the MGM Grand Hotel and Casino in Las Vegas. The MGM Grand was celebrating the fiftieth anniversary of the film, *It's a Wonderful Life,* starring Jimmy Stewart. Since the movie had an angel in it, they invited Marilynn, the Angel Lady, to be the keynote speaker for the event and sign her books. I will never forget the shock that came to me when I drove into Las Vegas and saw her name up in lights at the MGM Grand. I gasped and said, "I'm sure I am the only pastor whose wife is a headliner in Las Vegas!"

I don't remember when it began or who first called her "the Angel Lady". I do know it accurately reveals one of her passions: to glorify God by telling everyone she can about the heavenly hosts.

Chapter Two

Tea at Marilynn's

A guest shares her experience

Even the address, Celeste Drive, suggested the heavenly hosts. As we approached the house, a large angel-shaped flag fluttering in the breeze caught our attention. Then we noticed an angel weather vane on the roof and a six-foot topiary bush trimmed in the shape of Gabriel blowing his trumpet by the front door.

Looking for the doorbell, we were not surprised to find it in the shape of an angel as well. As the front door opened a music box played "The Wind Beneath My Wings." Marilynn Webber, the Angel Lady, greeted each guest personally. She was wearing a dress with an angel print and shoes covered with the same fabric. "Welcome to the house of angels!" she exclaimed warmly.

And angels were everywhere. A life-size kneeling angel, identical to the one found in the Pope's private chapel, graced the entry hall. The light fixture overhead was in the form of a flying cherub. Lladro, Boehm, and Kaiser angels filled the window shelf in the living room. The sofa was upholstered in a delicate angel pattern. Everywhere we saw evidence of the 4,000 angels in Marilynn's collection.

The guests were seated in the living room. In response to their questions, Marilynn recounted her experiences found in chapter one of this book, telling how her life-long interest in angels began when she was a small child, afraid of the dark.

In the kitchen, Marilynn's husband Bill has been busy with the preparations for the tea that can only be done at the last minute. As Marilynn chats with the guests, Bill served the first course. On this day the tea began with tea sandwiches, an individual quiche, celestial salad, lemon bread with lemon curd, and a mini-muffin. The plate was garnished with edible flowers from their own garden. The dishes are Coalport china made by Wedgewood, and the pattern was Revelry with a rim of cherubs, sold only in England. Marilynn discovered the china pattern at Harrod's Department Store in London when she and Bill were on an exchange pastorate in England. Tea is served from an angel teapot. Marilynn has a collection of angel teapots, and a different pot was used each time the cups were filled.

After the dishes were collected, Bill explained that the next course would be scones. From my seat in the living room I had been able to see into the kitchen, and I had watched as Bill had taken the scones from the oven just minutes before. Because many tea guests were not familiar with scones Bill explained their background and the etiquette of eating a scone. He told us that the British and Scots pronounce the word *scone* differently. The English generally say *scone* with a long o. In Scotland most people say the word as if it were spelled *scoon,* the same pronunciation they use for the Stone of Scone.

He told us that scones are traditionally served with jam and clotted cream from Devonshire, England. Today Bill had prepared a mock Devonshire cream which proved to be delicious. He explained that in the British Isles the etiquette for eating scones differs from region to region. Usually the scone is broken or sliced in half as if it were a dinner roll. In some areas the cream is spread first on the scone, then the jam; in other areas it is the jam that is spread first, then the cream. But in some places they insist that the only proper way to eat a scone is to break off one small piece and spread the cream and jam only on that bite. Bill assured us that in the United States we are much more relaxed about etiquette, and the basic rule is simply to enjoy.

Bill, known for his story telling ability, joined the group for the scone course. As they spread the cream and jam on their scones with miniature angel knives he related true stories telling how angels have been active in the world today.

Traditionally a tea ends with a sweet, and that is always true at Marilynn's. The dessert items change from tea to tea, but always they are topped with a cloud of whipped cream with a little sugar angel perched on top.

Next Marilynn made a grand entrance wearing a beautiful set of angel wings. With great pomp, she read a proclamation naming one of the guests as an honorary angel. She gave each guest an angel pin as a reminder of the occasion. "When you go to a Chinese restaurant, they give you a fortune cookie," she explained. "At our angel teas, we give you an angel message." Marilynn passed out tiny scrolls, each with a different message—the kind of message an angel might give. As the guests took turns reading their message aloud, the listeners commented on how they had observed the quality described on the scroll to be true in the life of the person who read the message. Often they would share recollections of warm memories of deeds they had observed. It was a wonderful time of affirmation.

At the conclusion of the tea the guests were free to wander through the house and view Marilynn's collection of thousands of angels—collectibles, ceramic figures, books, jewelry, and pictures. Angel objects were in every room of the house, including the angel bed and the handle for the flusher on the toilet. The first all angel store in the country is in one wing of her home, and many spent time looking and shopping. When the tea was over the group left reluctantly. The warmth of the experience was reflected in the spontaneous hugs given as each person left.

Planning for Teas

Chapter Three

Tea for One, Two, or a Few

Tea for One

Tea for me? Tea for one solitary person? Yes! It's a wonderful thing to do. Better yet, it is a marvelous habit to cultivate. After all, one is a whole number, and I have found that taking time for a personal tea is one of the most beneficial things I can do not only for myself but also for those who inhabit my personal world.

Tea for one, when properly done, is a form of rest that can be just as vital as sleep. This brief time of tranquility is an excellent way of fine tuning our lives and providing a period of readjusting between life's activities. I have found a majority of women share this need. Most of us have learned to plan our work. Too many of us have never learned to take seriously the importance of planning that part of our lives which is not work related. Making tea time a priority can be one of the wisest decisions a person can make.

You Deserve A Break Today

It's the law that employers must give employees who work an eight-hour shift not only time for lunch but also a ten-minute break in the morning and afternoon. The intent of the law is to safeguard the health and well being of the workers. Studies have shown that employees who take breaks get more work done in the day than those who work straight through. Of course the person who uses their break as a time to cram in as much personal business as possible defeats the entire purpose. They are the losers. Homemakers and women who are self-employed often do not realize the importance of taking breaks. When we have the freedom to set our own schedules we should be at least as kind to ourselves as the law requires employers to be to their employees.

Add A Bit of Loveliness to Your Life

If you are like me, it doesn't work to stop in the middle of the afternoon and collapse in a comfortable chair. It makes me feel sleepy, and when break time is over I find it hard to get up and get going. What works best for me is to plan a break in my afternoon activity where I set aside my work and clear my mind for a few minutes. Instead of doing nothing, I choose to do something that is relaxing and a change of pace. When I lived in England I discovered how delightful and refreshing afternoon tea could be. My friend, the author Emilie Barnes, agrees. She writes in her best selling book, *If Teacups Could Talk*, that the potential of teatime for stress reduction is enormous.

"Tea takes time—and that's part of the magic. You can't hurry it without losing something vital. The act of making and drinking tea forces us to slow down—and I truly believe our bodies and spirits are desperate to slow down from the frantic pace our culture sets for us today. People in our society don't like to wait, but you simply cannot hurry a good pot of tea."

First you must wait until the water is boiling. I like to use my electric tea kettle. If I'm just making tea for myself, it doesn't take long to for one cup of water to boil. When my husband joins me or when friends drop by for tea it takes a little longer for the pot to boil. While I'm waiting I set out the teacups and arrange a plate of cookies. Next it takes time for the tea to steep. That's a lovely three to five minutes, no longer or the tea gets bitter. If I'm alone, I carry the tray to my favorite chair and wait in peace, using the time to think or pray or just relax until the tea reaches its fragrant amber. If I'm with friends, this is a wonderful time to talk.

Emilie Barnes continues, "No, none of these things is absolutely necessary. You can always go back to microwaving water and fishing your cookie directly from the package. You can drink your tea standing up at the counter or gulp it as you run out the door. But again, you'll be missing the opportunity. You see, boiling water in a kettle is a part of a ritual. Arranging the tea tray is a part of a ritual. Preparing and enjoying tea is a ritual in itself. I love what my friend Yoli Brogger calls it: 'a ceremony of loveliness.' And I believe with all my heart that human beings crave ritual and ceremony (and loveliness) in our lives."

It's your choice. It may take time to learn to slow down, take a break from your hectic pace, and have a restful cup of tea for a few minutes restoring your soul, but I can guarantee that it is worth it.

Tea for Two

My husband and I are writers and speakers, and we both work at home. We have two priorities each day. One is our daily devotional time that begins each day, and the other is afternoon tea. We look forward to this break from the day's activity. Usually teatime is brief; only taking about fifteen minutes from the time the teakettle is set to boil to the time the cups are placed in the dishwasher. We have discovered the break actually helps us accomplish more in the afternoon, as well as being a wonderful way to nourish our relationship. For this short time work is set aside, the television is silent (but we may have quiet music playing), and we give our attention to taking tea and each other.

Normally we keep it simple. Often it is just the cup of tea. If we add a sweet we are careful to control the number of extra calories. Too much of a good thing can spoil one's appetite for the evening meal as well as gradually add extra pounds. We find it interesting to sample different varieties of tea. Sometimes we substitute a special coffee and may include a piece of biscotti for dipping. Our tea for two is meant to nourish the soul rather than the body.

We have found that teatime works best when we are both together to turn on our electric kettle. Sharing the simple chores involved with brewing the tea are important as they make a bridge from work or other activities and set the stage for quality time together. It would be possible for two people to simply sit and talk in the middle of the afternoon. However we have found the tea ritual, from boiling the water to the clean up, gives a sense of beginning and ending to our special time, and that conversation is aided when each of us sips a cup of tea.

Tea for Two or a Few

A tea also is a wonderful reason to invite a friend or a few friends to your home for the afternoon. You don't need an agenda or have a purpose to ask them to come. It's perfectly proper to call and simply say, "Would you join me for a cup of tea?" You can choose to be very simple in what you serve; scones and jam would be quite enough. I prefer to bake my own from scratch, but many stores have excellent scone mixes, and quite a few even have scones in their bakery section. But although scones are traditional in England, in the colonies a few cookies or teacakes will do very nicely. Of course, those things you prepare yourself are best, but there is nothing wrong in buying some goodies and using the extra time to prepare the table.

Yes indeed, you can be as fancy as you please. If you are celebrating a special life event for your friend, you may choose to be elaborate and formal. But always it is best to make the tea a catalyst, and keep the focus on your friend, not the food, and make conversation the main event.

Tea with Emilie

Remember you are celebrating friendship and enjoying tea, not showing off your culinary skills. I have learned that as long as that is your focus, your tea time will always be lovely, even if there is a disaster in the kitchen. I know, because this has happened to me. I had invited my friend, Emilie Barnes, to my home for a tea. Emilie is an authority on tea. She is the author of the best selling book *If Tea Cups Could Talk* and other tea books, and has spoken to thousands of women about tea. Perhaps she is most famous for her organizational skills. Her book *More Hours in Your Day* is the primer on how to organize your home and your life. On this day I wanted everything to be perfect. After all, for a tea in your home, Emilie is more Martha than Martha Stewart! My friend Carolynn Crowe had joined me in preparing a full cream tea with lovely sandwiches, scones, and sweets.

We were nearing the completion of our preparations when I began to preheat the oven for the scones. I was arranging the flowers on the table when I saw smoke billowing from the kitchen. When Carolynn and I rushed in we discovered the smoke was coming from the oven. Instantly I knew what had happened. The day before to make more counter space, I had slipped a plastic container in the cold oven. But I had forgotten. Now that plastic container had melted and was spewing vile smoke through the house. I pulled the rack out of the oven, and Carolynn rushed outside with it while I turned on the kitchen fan and opened all the windows. Smoke was already filling the house. It was a disaster. Carolynn and I burst into laughter. After all our work and planning there was no way this would be the perfect tea so we just relaxed and made the best of the situation. But was it a tragedy? No. Emilie was the one who laughed the hardest! That put us all at ease and after the smoke subsided we three had an unforgettable, warm tea time as friends.

Creative Ideas to Bring Friends Together for Tea

Celebrations

A tea is a warm and wonderful way to celebrate a birthday or mark a special event. Because an afternoon tea presupposes less food than a luncheon or a dinner, it takes less time and effort to prepare and keeps the focus on the guests. A birthday tea could simply be a pot of tea and a birthday cake. Or you could place a candle in any pastry or desert to create the effect. It can also be as elaborate as you choose to make it.

And why get together only to celebrate birthdays? Look for your friend's accomplishments and milestones and join together in celebrating them. Here are a few ideas to get you started: a new job or a promotion at work, completing a project, being in the newspaper, the birth of a grandchild, any good news, or a positive doctor's report.

An invitation to tea is also a gracious alternative a committee meeting. "We can plan that over a cup of tea at my house," is fun to say, and the response is usually enthusiastic. Suddenly the task has been transformed from a chore to a friendly gathering.

A Silver and Gold Tea

"Make new friends, but keep the old. One is silver and the other gold," the popular camp song goes. I have tried two variations on this theme and have found both work equally well. The first model I tried was to invite six women who were my friends but who did not know each other. What fun I had sharing the different interests I had in common with each one and telling the others what I found intriguing about them. This basic information primed the pump so it was easy for the guests to talk with each other and learn to know each other in a personal way. That was so much fun, I tried another angle. This time I invited three of my friends and asked each of them to invite one person I did not know. It was a great way for all of us to increase our circles of friendship.

I carried out theme by using a silver tablecloth with gold napkins. My centerpiece was a gold angel, and I found gold and silver place cards. I was glad to have an excuse to bring out my silver tea service. Other gold and silver items can be found in stores that carry items for weddings and anniversaries. I always prefer china for my teas, but you might choose to use silver paper plates and other accessories designed for the twenty-fifth or fiftieth wedding anniversaries.

Wear Purple with a Red Hat

I have just invited my friends to come to tea wearing a purple dress with a red hat. The invitations included the famous poem written by Jenny Joseph declaring that when she is an old woman she will do outrageous things. Why wait until we are old? The girls were delighted to receive such a scandalous invitation. Of course the tea cups will be mismatched, and each place setting will have a different napkin that will clash with the tablecloth, and for the centerpiece I will have purple flowers arranged in a teapot. I plan to push the envelope with the food I serve. For once it will be more humorous than elegant. I will use a cookie cutter to make my egg salad sandwiches round, then decorate them to look like faces with slices of olives for eyes and a red pimento slice for a mouth. There's egg in your face! I will read the poem, "When I am old, I shall wear purple with a red hat that doesn't suit me." Then everyone will share some outrageous thing they secretly would like to do when they are old enough not to worry about what other people think. I'm sorry you can't come, because everyone I invited jumped at the chance, so you will have to plan your own purple tea.

A Dress Up Tea

For a change of pace and lots of fun, invite your friends to dress for tea. They will enjoy picking out what to wear. Ask them to wear a hat and gloves, if possible. A Victorian dress would be perfect but not imperative. This would be an opportunity to bring out that really dressy dress that seems over the top for most occasions. Perhaps someone will even have a boa in the closet.

This is also a great idea for teens. When I visited my granddaughters, they invited me to be the guest of honor at a dress up tea they prepared for their friends. For the occasion our oldest grandchild, Aubrey, wore the elegant gown her mother had worn when our son Stephen won an Emmy. The other girls were equally splendid in their high heels, gowns, and jewelry borrowed from family members for the night. The girls loved the change from their usual casual attire, and the incongruity of the elegant apparel broke down inhibitions. I will always remember that delightful tea that bridged the generation gap so splendidly.

A Child's Tea

Children love tea parties! You can invite children to come for tea with their mothers, and they will feel very grown-up. Here are some things I have learned. Do use nice china cups. Perhaps not your priceless antiques, but if you trust the children with nice china at the tea, they will be careful, I promise! Perhaps more than anything else, using beautiful table service says to the child that they are doing something that is very special and very adult.

Best of all is the tea planned and prepared by children for children. Of course you can give guidance and help, but most of the tasks preparing for a tea can be done by a school aged child with the one exception of pouring the boiling water from the tea kettle if the child is very young.

Begin by planning the tea table. Setting the table for dinner may be a chore from a kid's point of view, but deciding how to make a table look elegant and unique is fun! Encourage creativity.

Let the young hostess make decisions about the menu. The adult can help the process by giving options and letting the younger partner choose between possibilities of things that are within their ability to make. Good choices include foods that children like but with a creative twist, like peanut butter and banana sandwiches. Another "cool" choice is the fluffernuter sandwich—peanut butter with marshmallow fluff. Or try the pinwheel recipe found in the recipe section of this book. It's great fun deciding what shapes and sizes to make the sandwiches, and using cookie cutters to fashion them. This is one time when it is proper to throw away the crusts! Sweets can include cookies the child has baked. Or perhaps cupcakes baked in flat-bottomed ice cream cones with the tops iced and covered with sprinkles.

And why not pretend? Our grandchildren love to make believe they are at a tea with the rich and famous. In their teatime chatter they fabricate stories about times they have had taking tea with the queen in the palace. Each flight of fancy leads to another. I have never hard such wonderful gossip.

Chapter Four

Have Tea Cup, Will Travel

Jim and Louise Weir have been friends for years. Now Louise was housebound, slowly recuperating from surgery. What could I do to brighten her day? "Let's have tea with Louise and Jim," I suggested to my husband.

"But she isn't feeling strong enough to go out, not even to our house," my husband objected.

"Then let's have tea at her house," I countered.

"But that would mean she would have to prepare the tea," my friend husband protested.

"Why don't we do the work and bring the tea to her?" I proposed. "We could pack it in a basket like a picnic. Only I will use one of my pretty baskets. We could prepare some teacakes and cookies and cover them with plastic wrap. I could pack four tea cups, four plates, and pretty napkins." I was getting more excited as the idea grew. "You could wrap one of my angel tea pots in bubble paper so it could make the trip without getting chipped."

"Yes, we could," Bill replied. "We would have to be careful that we didn't stay too long or we would tire her out."

I was already dialing the Weir's telephone number. Her husband answered the phone. "Jim, this is Marilynn. How is Louise feeling? Would she be up to a short visit tomorrow?"

"She is coming along slowly," Jim replied. "Being in this long has been difficult for her. I know it would help her if you could drop by."

"Tell her we will come at 2:30 for tea." I was certain Jim could hear the enthusiasm in my voice. "Tell her we will bring everything, even the tea cups. Jim, could you have a pot of water boiling when we arrive?"

"I sure could," he replied.

"And tell her we will just be there for only thirty minutes so we wont tire her too much," I added. "See you tomorrow!"

When we arrived the next day Louise was already seated at the kitchen table. A teakettle whistled merrily on the kitchen stove. Bill opened the basket we had prepared, unpacked the teapot, filled it with boiling water, and placed three tea bags in the pot to steep. By the time the tea was ready I had set out the teacups and taken the plastic wrap off the goodies. I folded the pretty angel napkins and put one at each plate.

"Bill will you say a prayer?" Louise asked.

Bill gave thanks for our friendship, for the tea, and prayed earnestly for her healing.

"This has brought such a bright spot to my day," Louise enthused. "And tea is so good for my recovery."

Then the retired couple shared their news. Their next-door neighbor was a second grade school teacher. Louise had made seasonal decorations for their schoolroom, and the children had voted to make them honorary grandparents. "I never heard of such a thing," Louise confided. We could tell she was thrilled with the unusual honor.

After thirty minutes we repacked our basket, said our farewells, and returned home. It was great fun, and we had been blessed.

On the drive home I remarked to my husband, "I think we've stumbled on to something, What a creative way to make a visit! Bringing tea makes a visit more delightful. It gives us something to do when we arrive, and helps conversation flow."

"Telling them we would be there for only thirty minutes was a stroke of genius on your part," Bill complimented. "It let them know what to expect. Louise didn't worry about becoming too tired. And with our busy schedules, it helped us leave gracefully. We will have to bring our moveable tea to more of our friends."

We did. Shut-ins have loved being a part of our afternoon teas. Next came the realization that tea-to-go was something that could be shared with almost anyone, anywhere. We have packed our tea basket to celebrate birthdays and anniversaries. It has been a fun way to make a friendly visit with new friends and old. It is a perfect way to mark special occasions where a party would seem to be too much. It can be a "hello" tea or a "goodbye" tea. At times it can almost be sacramental.

A few years ago Dr. Kok, the head of the Pastoral Care Department of the Crystal Cathedral, asked me to teach a class on angels. Through this I came to know and love Wendy and Donna, two of the workers in the pastoral care ministry. Through the years they became close friends and prayer partners. It was with a heavy heart that I learned that Wendy's husband was being transferred to Texas. Her church would miss her ministry, but I would miss my friend. I learned that Donna was scheduled for surgery and would be off work for several weeks.

I called Wendy and Donna at the Crystal Cathedral and asked if we could bring our tea to their office for their afternoon break. They checked with Dr. Kok, and then set the date for a Friday afternoon. Donna and Wendy had worked side by side for years. This would be their last day together on the job.

It was before Christmas, so when we packed our tea basket we included some of my favorite Swedish cookies. Even the sugar cubes were gaily decorated for the occasion. We made the 45-minute drive to the Crystal Cathedral, took our decorated basket from the trunk of the car, and made our way to the tower that housed the church offices. It was 2:30 when we stepped off the elevator in the pastoral care department. The staff greeted us warmly. Everyone knew we were coming at break time with tea for Wendy and Donna.

Donna hurried to bring the hot water for the tea. "Dr. Kok said we are to use his office," Wendy told us. It was a gracious setting for a tea. The windows overlooked the Crystal Cathedral shimmering in the sun. By the time the tea had brewed we had emptied our basket and set the conference table with china, silver, napkins, and dishes of assorted goodies.

Conversation began with comments about the angel teapot, plates, and goodies. Soon we were sharing on a deeper level. Wendy had been asked to speak at the next staff meeting, and she had been working on her talk. Would we help? She outlined her ideas: her first impressions when she began working at the Crystal Cathedral, a humorous incident or two, but most of all the inspiring times and high and holy moments of her seven years of ministry.

Donna spoke of her coming surgery. She shared her apprehension and her faith. We talked about the recovery time of several weeks. Because Donna's surgery was Monday and Wendy was moving to Texas, this was the last day the two would be working together. The tea became a termination ritual for two friends who were closing this chapter in their lives. We ended with fervent prayers. It was a beautiful closure for Wendy and Donna. We had been privileged to be a part of it.

How to Prepare a Tea to Go

We found a beautiful heart-shaped basket that was just the right size to hold all the items we would bring for a tea. We learned how pretty tea towels could be used to pack and protect the cups, plates, and teapots. We found that fragile cookies travel best when they are packed in a small tin. A mini loaf of date-nut bread needs only to be covered with plastic wrap. It is always appreciated when we leave any of the loaf that was not used with those we visit. At first we forgot to bring sweetening for the tea. Now we bring packets of artificial sweetener (very practical) and some sugar cubes (for a touch of teatime elegance). Pretty napkins are a must. I usually bring angel napkins. Here is the one place where paper will do. I always avoid paper plates. A proper tea calls for china plates and cups. I choose nice dishes, although they are not my very best. I have never had any problems with anything breaking. For special times I leave a teacup as a gift. Instead of taking time from the visit to do the dishes, we just empty the cups and teapot, then wipe them dry with paper towels we have brought along, and pack them in our basket.

A "tea to go" has been a blessing to many, but I have been the one most richly blessed.

A Telephone Tea

My husband Bill sensed my unhappiness. I had just finished reading a letter that had come in the afternoon mail from best-friend Ruth Smith with the news that her multiple sclerosis was growing worse and restricting her activities even more. "How I wish I could have a cup of tea with Ruth and give her a little encouragement," I said to Bill.

"That's a great idea," my husband, the eternal optimist, replied. "Just do it."

"I can't just do it," I objected. "Ruth lives hundreds of miles away. The best I can do is to talk to her on the telephone, but having tea together would be so much warmer."

Suddenly an idea burst into my mind. "Do you think we could have tea over the telephone?" I asked.

Bill looked puzzled, but he knew I was serious. "Tell me what you are thinking," he prodded.

"We take a tea in a basket to our friends who live near us. Why couldn't we pack the same things in a box and mail it to Ruth? We could put in some tea bags, some nice sweets, napkins of course, and why not even send her a teacup? I would call Ruth on the telephone and tell her the box was coming. Then Ruth and I would choose a time to do tea over the telephone. If we picked two o'clock Tuesday I would have tea ready in my home when I made the phone call and Ruth would be waiting for my call with her teacup and goodies ready. Let's do it!"

It was fun preparing the tea in a box. It was fun for Ruth to anticipate receiving this unusual package in the mail. But most delightful of all was the time we spent chatting and sipping tea. Unlike a regular telephone call our telephone tea was a real visit. Best of all it gave Ruth something to look forward to, and an unusual experience instead of an ordinary telephone call. In a tangible way it showed her I really cared.

Since that time I have enjoyed teatime on the telephone with many of my friends who live at a distance. It has always proved to be the highlight of both of our days.

Try It. You Will Like It!

Because bringing tea in a basket or doing a telephone tea is so much fun I just had to share the idea when talking to friends. I have also included it in presentations and talks I have made to groups. Some of the women present have taken the idea, given it their own personal twist, and found it to be a blessing. Some groups have developed a tea ministry as a welcome way to keep in touch with members who are unable to get out. And I learned I was not the first to think of bringing tea in a basket. It is such a good idea that others, quite independently, have come up with the same idea much to the joy and delight of their teatime companions.

There is something special about having tea with a friend. Don't let distance, poor health, or other factors keep you from nurturing your friendships.

Chapter Five

How to Plan and Serve a Tea for a Large Group

Tea is in! An expert on trends predicts that tea will become the drink of the millennium. I first noticed the growing interest in Southern California. As a break from the ordinary, women were going out to tea. The places serving afternoon tea were multiplying. Women would drive for miles in order to take tea at places like the elegant Ritz Carlton Hotel in Laguna Niguel. Soon many upscale hotels and restaurants were offering afternoon teas. Then lovely old Victorian mansions began teatime and discovered an enthusiastic response. Teahouses began to appear to meet the growing demand. Tea societies were formed, and a guidebook listing hundreds of places offering tea in Southern California quickly sold out its first printing.

Next I noticed a growing trend when a program chairwoman would call and ask me to present a program for their church group. In the past the request usually had been for me to speak at their banquets or luncheons. Now more and more groups were having teas, and the response to the teas was for the most part enthusiastic.

Not always. Just announcing a tea will not bring out the women, and serving tea instead of coffee does not in itself create a delightful experience. I drove one day to a beautiful church in Los Angeles to give the program for their spring tea. I allowed myself extra driving time to compensate for any problems on the Los Angeles freeways. When I arrived at the church a half-hour early I found one woman in the kitchen beginning to fill a large coffee urn with the water they would use to make tea. From experience I knew that it would take more than 30 minutes for the water to heat in an urn of that size, so I asked if the program would be presented before the refreshments. "Oh, no," came the cheerful reply. "We always eat first. It will take some time for this water to get ready, but the girls always come late and we never start on time."

Just as predicted the women straggled in. Making the best of the situation, I enjoyed chatting with them as they arrived. About ten minutes after the scheduled starting time two of the women disappeared into the kitchen and returned with Styrofoam cups, napkins, and plastic tableware which they placed on what I surmised would be the serving table. There was no centerpiece. The room in which they met was attractive, but generic, apparently unchanged since a Sunday School class had met there days before.

I discovered I was not the only one who was wondering when the tea would begin. "Hasn't Mabel gotten here yet?" one of my new friends asked in a voice that indicated it was addressed to the entire group.

"No, not yet," a voice answered from across the room. "She had to stop by the grocery store to buy the cookies for our tea. She should be here any minute now." Almost as if on cue Mabel bustled in the room, then retreated into the kitchen to find some paper plates for the cookies.

"The water is ready, girls," called the woman I had met in

the kitchen, as she placed a couple of teapots filled with hot water on the serving table. Mabel added her plates of cookies, and the women gathered around to serve themselves. "We need some sugar," one of them observed, and Mabel hurried into the kitchen to find the sugar bowl.

I waited in line for my turn at the table. Mabel's choice of store bought cookies was remarkably ordinary, with Oreos easily being the most attractive. They must have been Mabel's favorites because they outnumbered the other cookies. I placed an Oreo on my paper plate, filled a cup with hot water, took a tea bag and a plastic spoon, and returned to my place to brew my tea.

"I'm really disappointed at the turnout today," volunteered the woman sitting next to me. "We decided to have a tea because we heard that people turn out for teas. I guess that's not true of our church, though," she added sadly. "We are having fewer women attend our meetings every year."

This is a true story. I have not exaggerated. The women were sincere. I liked the people I had met. But as an outsider I could easily see their problem. There were no expectations for their meeting. No one anticipated anything other than the ordinary. They came expecting little, and their expectations became reality. Those who had attended in the past had dropped out feeling they were not missing anything. Changing the name of their monthly meeting to a "tea" did not work magic.

Doing Tea Properly

I have been the speaker for many churches where teas were enthusiastically received. Often their meeting rooms were filled to capacity, and several women's groups found it necessary to have a waiting list. In each case there were several factors that created interest and excitement. Here are tested ideas your church or group can use.

Let the Women Know This Event Will Be Special

Capitalize on the current interest in tea. The members of your group are waiting for something interesting to do that is a break from their regular routine. This is especially true of those you would like to reach but never attend. Don't hesitate to "advertise." You are filling a need. Let them know how this day in their life can be special. Carefully plan how you will make the announcement of the coming tea in your meeting. Choose a person to speak who will be enthusiastic and create excitement among the women. Tell them about some of the features that will be different and intriguing.

Give thought to other ways to publicize your meeting. How can an article in your church newsletter create interest? Can someone design a poster that will point to the uniqueness and elegance of the coming event? More important than posters, newsletter, and announcements is word of mouth. Give the girls something to talk about and they will spread the word.

Encourage the Women to Dress for Tea

Ask the women to dress, wear hats and even gloves if they can find them. Part of the attraction for your event is that it flies contrary to the current trends of being casual and anything goes. The girls who always dress casually are the ones most likely to join in the fun and may even come wearing a boa!

Involvement Creates Interest

The easiest way to involve the most people is to ask them to bring their own teacup. Explain that it was the custom in Victorian times for each woman to bring their own cup when they came for tea. Ask them to select a cup that is beautiful or has special meaning for them. Tell them they will have the opportunity to share with the others at their table why they chose to bring this specific cup. If teacups could talk they would have interesting stories to tell. The owners of the teacups also have much to share. The cup may have belonged to a favorite grandmother, been a gift from a special friend, bought as a souvenir, or be treasured simply for its beauty. My heart has been warmed when I have observed conversations around the table as people shared memories evoked by their teacups. I have seen warmth, joy, laughter, and sentimental tears in this beautiful but nonthreatening time.

Another creative activity is to have someone choose one teacup from each table for special recognition. The cups may be chosen for beauty, uniqueness, or sentimental value. Several times I have been asked to be the judge since I came from a distance as the speaker of the day and would be able to be impartial in the choice. How interesting the task has been! What fun and laughter I have enjoyed as I moved from table to table, meeting interesting people with intriguing anecdotes to tell.

Speaking of Teacups

When I presented the program for a large Presbyterian Church tea, each woman found a different cup at her place. These became a topic of conversation. Imagine their surprise when they were told the teacups were a gift to remind them of the tea and that they could take them home with them. Two women from the church had started a year before the event to shop for the cups. They had a great time going to antique stores, flea markets, and garage sales looking for nice cups they could purchase at a reasonable price. When they explained what they were doing shop owners often gave them tremendous bargains on cups that had been in the shop for a long time and had not sold.

How to Have Dazzling Decorations Without Cost

An idea that offers great rewards is to assign a different person to decorate each table. This hostess will be responsible for the tablecloth, china, place settings, and centerpiece. It is not a difficult assignment since each woman has only one table to decorate. In most cases she already has in her house everything she needs to set the table. If she decides to make or purchase a centerpiece for the occasion, she can bring it home after the function and reuse it for entertaining at home.

This has become a tradition at the world famous Crystal Cathedral in Southern California for their annual Christmas dinners. Although their program is always world class and the food is superb, the splendor of the decorated tables is probably the greatest drawing card for this always sold-out event. Viewing the tables is such an enjoyment the women come early to the dinner so they can spend time admiring each arrangement.

Don't miss the important lesson to be learned from the Crystal Cathedral. Your church may not be as large or famous as the Crystal Cathedral, you may not be able to afford a world class program, but your women can decorate tables. Shortly after I presented the Christmas program for the women at the Crystal Cathedral I was the speaker for a Christmas tea at a church in a small town in the state of Washington. They had followed the same plan, and to my surprise and delight their tables were equally as stunning as the ones at the Crystal Cathedral.

This idea is not only for Christmas. Through the year I speak at church teas, brunches, lunches, and banquets and find that the idea can be used at any season. It can be successful for a spring affair, for mother-daughter occasions, to begin the fall season, or for any other event. There is one caution, however. It will loose its specialness if repeated too often. If you expect the women to be creative and outstanding with the table decorations, do not schedule this activity more than once a year.

Consider the benefits of this approach. The first is that it involves many women in the preparation for your tea. It gives an opportunity to include women who enjoy setting a pretty table but might not otherwise be active in your group. It gives them an opportunity to use their special china and silver that are seldom used in our casual age. You will also discover that these women are proud they were asked and are talking with their friends about the plans for "their table." Many will invite friends who do not attend the same church to be their guests and sit at their table. This kind of invitation is far more personal and successful than simply asking them to attend the meeting.

Instead of overworking a few members of the decorating committee, this plan shares the task among many. Because they are responsible for only one table, no one is overworked. This is also the most economical approach because each woman supplies what is needed for her table. Usually she will gladly share some of her "treasures" from her home, thankful that some wider use has been found for them. "After all, what is the use of having beautiful things if you have no opportunity to use them?" more than one woman has said to me. These treasures may be heirlooms, but they could just as well be the handwork of a crafter. A woman who has the gift of growing and arranging flowers may use a beautiful bouquet from her garden as the focal point. Others may use items from their collection to decorate the table. I often see tables filled with beautiful angels when I speak on my book *A Rustle of Angels.* When I talk on "Me and My Teddy Bear" many exceptional bears come out of hibernation from their mistresses' homes to grace the banquet tables.

The Advantages of Tickets

As I have spoken at hundreds of churches, I have discovered the groups with the largest attendance sell tickets. At first I was puzzled. Wouldn't more people come if it were free, I reasoned? As I talked with the leaders they explained why tickets are effective. First, the woman who purchases a ticket makes a definite decision to attend. Secondly, no one wants to waste money. So if there are other things to do or the weather turns bad, people still use their ticket and come. I was to speak at a tea in one of the northern states. The day began with a cold rain that turned to hail and then snow. Two hundred tickets had been sold. Two hundred six women showed up. Women who were sick gave their tickets to a friend. Everyone wanted to be certain her ticket was used. The price of the ticket was only five dollars. A ticket does not have to be expensive to be effective. Even if the ticket costs only one dollar it will still boost attendance.

Tickets have other advantages. It makes it easier for some people to invite guests when they tell them they have bought a ticket for them. It helps the committee know how many are coming. If a list is kept of those who have purchased tickets, nametags can be prepared in advance. Adding a few dollars to the ticket can cover the cost of food, decorations, and the program.

Advantages of a Tea for a Church Group

There are several benefits for planning a tea instead of a luncheon. First, teas are popular today. A tea suggests elegance, an experience that will be a cut above the ordinary. This can lead to a larger group being present.

Although it is special, in many ways preparing for a tea is simpler than preparing a meal at the church. The easiest way, of course, is to have your function catered. Some of the most beautiful affairs I have spoken at were catered teas. The cost is greater when a tea is catered, but if you have access to a good caterer it can be a delightful change. A tea can also be catered successfully by someone who is not a professional, perhaps a member of your group. A tea may also be less expensive to cater than a full meal. A caterer can be a good choice if you are meeting in a hall without good kitchen facilities.

But you can also prepare your own tea even with a very limited or no kitchen at all. I have a friend with a successful tearoom in an antique shop that has no kitchen. All her food is prepared in her kitchen at home and brought to the tearoom.

Another advantage of a tea is that many people can share in the preparation of the food at their own schedule without any one person being overworked. Here's how it works. Have the committee decide on a menu. There are plenty of choices to be found in the recipe section of this book. Recruit four or five people to make small attractive tea sandwiches. Each will make only one kind. Doing one sandwich in quantity makes it easy to prepare, even when elegant garnishes are added. Most sandwiches can be made in advance and refrigerated or frozen until the day they are served. The sandwiches are moister and improve in quality if you follow the directions for freezing or refrigeration found in the recipe section of this book

In the same way different individuals may be assigned to make scones, savories, and sweets using the recipes in this book with each cook preparing only one item. All of the items at a tea may be prepared ahead of time without the need to reheat them and keep them warm. Of course, it is also possible to serve warm savories (I often serve individual quiches), but this is completely at the discretion of the planning group. Remember that fruit and salad are also appropriate for a tea.

In many churches the women prepare the tea on site. The food may be simple, yet still be elegant. The menu could be a croissant filled with chicken salad and a fruit salad with a garnish of grapes. Cookies or one of the sweets chosen from the recipe section in this book could complete the tea.

Or you may decide to serve a splendid tea with many items. In that case, a group of women can have a wonderful time in the church kitchen creating beautiful tea sandwiches and other delicacies they have chosen to be on their menu. Don't hesitate to use this plan simply because the church kitchen is small. Unlike other meal functions you do not need to use the stoves and ovens. The tables in the church fellowship hall can be used, making the entire fellowship hall a large kitchen for the day.

How to Serve Tea to a Large Group

If your group is small, you will be able to follow the directions for making the perfect cup of tea found in the recipe section of this book. This simply is not practical for large meetings. I have discovered that even tea societies find alternate methods to brew large amounts of tea. Try one of the following.

If the occasion is served buffet style then one or more women can "pour". It adds style and elegance to use silver teapots. If the group is large have several women pour to be able to serve the group quickly. Some women will be delighted to bring their silver tea service from home for the occasion, thankful that they were able to find a use for their lovely wedding present.

If the guests are seated at a table it is always possible to serve tea from a pitcher. It is considerably more fitting and interesting to use teapots, however. A nice thing about borrowing teapots for your event is that every pot is likely to be different. This makes it easy for each woman to claim her own pot after the tea.

Tea is best when it is brewed from water that has just come to a boil. The longer the water boils, the more oxygen is released. The ideal would be to warm the pots by filling them with hot water. Then when it is time to serve the tea, empty the warm water from the first teapot and immediately fill it with boiling water from the kettle, and add the teabags (usually three). Let the tea steep for at least three minutes but no more than five minutes or the tea may begin to become bitter. It is easier to discard the tea bags in the kitchen then at the table. If each table is to discard their tea bags, be sure to provide a dish for the spent tea bags. Since tea is at its best when hot, try to bring the pots to the tables immediately.

A second alternative is to have tea bags on the table. A delightful touch is to provide an assortment, including flavored and herbal teas in a basket that is passed. When pots of boiling water are brought in from the kitchen, each woman brews her own cup of tea. If you choose this method be sure the teapot holds enough hot water to fill every cup on the table or have a method so the pots can be quickly refilled. Most of your guests will want more than one cup of tea so refilling the pot at some time is a necessity. Because the water in the pot will cool down, the wise hostesses bring fresh pots of boiling water midway through the tea.

Believe it or not, modern technology has provided a truly workable solution for tea with a large group. There are now liquid concentrates available that provide the quality of brewed tea with the convenience of instant. The liquid concentrates far outclass the powdered instant teas. Liquid concentrates can be found in many of the better grocery stores as well as gourmet shops.

Even better is a liquid concentrate you make yourself. Penny Carlevato of Penelope's Tea Time in El Segundo, California prefers this method. Here are her instructions:

Place 1/3 to1/2 cup of loose tea in a pot. Pour 1 quart of boiling water over the tea leaves and steep 3 to 6 minutes. Strain the tea and discard the tea leaves. This concentrate may be made ahead of time and kept refrigerated.

For a large group, before the tea begins, line up all the teapots on the countertop in the kitchen. Following the directions, place the amount of liquid concentrate in each pot (usually about 1/2 ounce). When the time comes to serve the tea, fill the pots with hot water and take them directly to the tables. It is a decided advantage that it is not necessary to use boiling water, although the hotter the better. Water from a large coffee urn will do quite nicely since the tea does not have to brew. A nice touch: use a little less concentrate and put one tea bag in each pot for the visual effect. Have the server bring the pot to the table with the tag still peeking out from under the lid.

When serving tea, it is necessary to have sugar, artificial sweeteners, and a pitcher of milk on the table. While Americans often add cream to coffee, milk is the appropriate addition to tea.

Serving a spiced tea eliminates the need for sweeteners and milk. It is a delightful beverage to serve especially at a Christmas tea.

The Three Basic Ways to Serve the Food

An excellent choice for serving tea sandwiches, scones, and other items on your menu is to prepare the plates in the kitchen. Women loved to be served, and this is a good option if you have enough workers to prepare and serve the plates. Remember this takes time and artistry. It is entirely different than many church dinners where all that is expected is the placing scoops of meat, potatoes, and veggies on a dinner plate. A tea plate should be arranged with beauty, and this takes time. Fortunately most tea plates can be prepared in advanced if the food is kept covered to keep the tea sandwiches from drying out. Many churches enlist the men to be servers for their special functions. If so, the arrangement of the food on the plates should not be left to the individual servers. This should be done by a small group of people who have the talent for making the plates look pretty. Many men can do this as well as women. The point is that not everyone has the gift, and at a tea presentation it is especially important.

Often the servers who are recruited are very willing but unclear about their specific duties or when to do each task. I presented the program for a very gracious tea at a Lutheran Church. The committee had planned to have the program immediately after the dessert course before the tables were cleared. During the program the men of the church who were the servers would eat their meal and have the opportunity for fellowship. Unfortunately the committee had not communicated their plan clearly to the men. At the most solemn place in my talk where the full attention of the group was most important, the principal of the church school (a very godly man) accompanied by his six-year-old son entered the room and noisily began to clear the tables. This could have been avoided if the instructions had been clearly given. Pam, one of my friends who is in constant demand to cater teas, has found the ideal way to solve this and other problems. She writes a detailed list of what each server is to do, when it is to be done, and instructions on how it is to be done. She posts this list in several conspicuous places in the kitchen and preparation areas. It avoids confusion and it greatly appreciated by the amateur workers who return to check the instructions over and over to be certain they are following the plan.

A second option is to arrange the food items on serving plates to be passed around the table. There may be one or more plates of sandwiches, another plate may have scones, and others may have the other menu items. The guests may choose to take one of each item or may pass some things by. This allows the women to choose according to their individual tastes and gives them the opportunity to eat lightly if they are counting calories. An elegant way to serve in this style is to use three tiered serving dishes popular in tea houses, if you can find enough of them to go around. Take care with the presentation, and arrange the sandwiches and other food so that everything looks lovely. A tea plate often uses edible flowers for garnish, such as pansies.

A third option is to serve buffet style. The food may be presented, beautifully arranged, on one or more tables. Usually it is best to replenish the food as the women serve themselves. A tea lends itself to this. For example, when the plate of cucumber sandwiches (very British) is almost empty it is replaced with a fresh plate. When serving buffet style, be aware that it takes some women a long time to make choices, especially if there is a wide array of food items. For a large group it is best to have more than one serving table and to set these up so that the women can serve themselves from both sides of the table.

Tea Etiquette

What is proper at a tea? Tea etiquette varies widely. In some places in England it is proper to spread the Devon cream on a scone before one spreads the jam. In other localities they insist the only proper way is to spread the jam first, then the cream. In other areas, the etiquette is that one must spread only enough jam and cream for one bite.

Which is correct? Some churches have invited a tea expert to bring a program on tea and its etiquette. Their next meeting is the tea itself, with all the members feeling at ease with the manners and social graces that have been agreed upon. Dana Mae Casperson is perhaps the leading authority on tea in the United States, presenting the protocol of tea at sessions in the leading hotels and for tea societies. She offers this clear, common sense advice. "The basic rule of doing tea is to delight in the experience. In the United States following a set of rules or prescribed rituals is not as important as simply enjoying the tea."

What great advice! Don't fret about details. Just have a wonderful time at your tea.

Chapter Six

Favorite Tea Recipes

How to Brew A Perfect Cup of Tea

When or wherever you have your next cup of tea, tomorrow's breakfast, in the evening, or over ice with the kids after they've come home from school, there are some simple steps to follow to make the tea properly.

By the Pot...

Use freshly drawn cold water. To begin, always let tap water run for a few seconds until it is nice and cold. This way you'll be sure the water is completely aerated (full of oxygen), necessary for bringing out your tea's full flavor.

Remove the water after a full, rolling boil. You want your water completely hot, but don't let it boil too long. Doing so would boil away some of that flavor releasing oxygen, resulting in flat tasting tea.

Preheat your *teapot.* Temperature is very important for brewing tea properly, and that's why tea lovers take the extra step of preheating their teapot before use. To do so, simply fill the teapot with very hot water and let it stand for a few minutes.

Use one tea bag or teaspoon per cup. Place the tea bags in your preheated teapot, allowing one tea bag per cup of tea you're steeping. If you're using loose tea rather than tea bags, simply measure one teaspoon per cup. You can put the loose tea in the bottom of the pot or use a tea infuser or tea ball. Just be sure the device is large enough to allow the tea to expand and brew properly.

Brew three to five minutes. Pour the boiled water into your teapot and immediately cover to retain heat. During the next three to five minutes, the full flavor, color, and body of the tea will be released, and then your perfect cups of tea are ready to serve. Don't make the mistake of steeping more than five minutes. This would produce a bitter flavor.

Serve it *to taste.* Some of us like our tea with lemon, others with milk and sugar, and others enjoy a combination. Honey is also a popular accompaniment to many teas, particularly herbals. In the end, the perfect cup of tea is a matter of personal preference. Whatever your tea preference, refrain from adding cream instead of milk. Most everyone agrees cream masks tea's flavor.

Or By the Cup

You can have equally delicious tea if you're brewing it by the cup - as long as you follow the same basic directions for pot brewing. To review, be sure to bring cold water to a rolling boil, but do not overboil. Pour the water over the tea bag in the cup and let it steep three to five minutes. Try not to give in to the temptation of drinking your tea before it's had at least three full minutes to steep, even if it looks dark enough to drink. You shouldn't judge tea's readiness by color. Full taste requires three to five minutes of steeping. Whenever possible, cover the cup to retain the heat while your tea is steeping. Your saucer will do the job nicely.

"Drinking tea in the afternoon is like giving yourself a vacation," writes Gale Gand, who daily prepared tea in an English country hotel. "The thing about tea is that it should be both lovely and filled of surprises, much like opening a box of treasured Christmas ornaments, each with it's own story and history. Tea foods are little bursts of flavor, and small serving sizes mean you can try everything."

Professional Tips on Making Sandwiches

Tea sandwiches should be a joy to behold and an adventure to eat. They are elegant, and very light—fragile morsels, not intended to be a meal in themselves. Because they are dainty, it is a tradition to present an assortment of tea sandwiches, arranged to be a visual delight. Tea sandwiches are special occasion fare. Their shapes should be different, and the sampler should include some delightful variations from the ordinary sandwich fillings.

It is best to begin with unsliced bread, homemade if possible. If bread is a day old, it is still fresh but much easier to work with. Slice the bread very thin. Use an electric knife if you have one. For most sandwiches, before adding the filling, spread one side of each slice to the very edges with softened butter, whether or not you will be using mayo or cream cheese. Butter acts like the bread's little raincoat and keeps it from getting soggy. Because the slices are thin, you will find it easier to spread each slice before you cut it from the loaf. An alternative spread is two parts softened butter beaten together with one part mayonnaise. This spreads very easily and makes a subtle base for many fillings.

First assemble the sandwiches, then cut off the crusts. Next cut the sandwiches into the desired shapes. For variety, leave some sandwiches open-faced to show off the fillings. Pinwheel sandwiches also add to the visual impact of the plate.

Be creative with breads. In addition to white and wheat, use marbled rye, dark pumpernickel, and raisin nut breads. Specialty breads, such as lemon bread, make an interesting variation, and complement many spreads.

Sandwiches are best made the day of the party. They can be prepared the day before if they are properly wrapped and stored. We use an airtight container (Tupperware or similar). Place a moist towel in the bottom. Fill the container with the sandwiches, then cover with the moist towel, taking care to see that every part is covered. Seal the container and place in the refrigerator overnight. Even sandwiches made the same day will profit from being wrapped this way. The damp towel will keep the bread moist. Be sure the towel is not wet or the bread will become soggy. When you get ready to party keep the sandwiches covered, even on trays, until they are ready to be eaten. Bread dries out quickly when exposed to the air. The most elegant sandwich prepared with the greatest care will lose much of its quality if the bread is allowed to dry out. This is the most common failing at teas.

CUCUMBER SANDWICHES (GRATED)

1 cucumber
1 (8 ounce) package cream cheese
dash of salt
1/8 teaspoon horseradish

Slice end off cucumber. Remove and discard seeds from center. Using a medium grater, grate the cucumber. Mix with softened cream cheese, salt, and horseradish.

A dash of lemon juice may be substituted for the horseradish.

Marilynn often uses this as the filler for her harlequin sandwiches.

CUCUMBER SANDWICHES (SLICED)

Mrs. Beeton's Family Cookery

1 large cucumber
creamed butter
white or brown bread
salad oil
lemon juice or vinegar
salt and pepper

Peel the cucumber, slice it thinly. Season liberally with salt. Drain on a sieve for about 1 hour and dry thoroughly. Put it into a basin and sprinkle with pepper, salad oil, lemon juice or vinegar, according to taste. Have ready some thin slices of bread and butter, stamp out some rounds of suitable size, place slices of cucumber between 2 rounds of bread, and press the parts well together. Or serve open face. Dish lightly overlapping each other in a circle on a folded napkin, and serve with parsley.

HARLEQUIN FINGERS

1/2 of 1 pound unsliced loaf of white bread
1/2 of 1 pound unsliced loaf of wheat bread
1/2 cup butter, room temperature
8 ounces cream cheese
8 ounces pimento cheese

Cut each loaf into thin slices. Lightly spread butter and cream cheese on 1 slice. Spread butter and pimento cheese on the second slice. Spread butter and cream cheese on the third slice. Stack slices, filling side up, alternating white and wheat, making 3 layers of bread. Top with a slice that has no spread for the fourth layer.

Wrap in foil and refrigerate 1 hour. The butter will harden and keep the slices together. Remove from the refrigerator and trim the crusts. Cut stacks into strips about 1/2 inch wide, slicing through all 4 layers. Display on plates with the stripe side up. Makes about 30 fingers. Note: Made from contrasting colors of bread, these two tone sandwiches take their name from the striped costumes of the harlequins.

FANCY PINWHEEL SANDWICHES

1 pound loaf of unsliced day-old white bread (fresh bread will be difficult to cut)
1/2 cup butter, room temperature
Use any soft filling. Pimento cheese is fun. Plain cream cheese can be used. Egg or tuna salad will also work well if spread thinly. For the children, use creamy peanut butter.

Neatly cut off all crusts from loaf of bread. Lightly spread butter to edges of one long side. Cut length-wise into as thin a slice as possible. Spread buttered side of slice with filling. Roll up lengthwise, jelly-roll style. Wrap in foil. Repeat until loaf is finished—you should have about 6 rolls. Refrigerate for at least an hour so butter will harden and hold rolls together. Just before serving, cut each roll crosswise in about 5 slices. Makes about 30 pinwheels.

SALMON PINWHEELS

1-1⁄2 cups cold poached salmon (or 1 pound can of salmon)
1⁄4 cup mayonnaise
salt, pepper and lemon juice to taste
unsliced loaf of bread

Cut the loaf into a rectangular cube, removing the crusts. Slice bread loaf lengthwise, three times. Spread evenly with butter. Spread evenly with salmon (filling), leaving 1⁄2-inch border uncovered on one long side. Roll up tightly from the side opposite the 1⁄2-inch border. Make into a cylinder. Wrap in waxed paper, then in damp tea towel. Refrigerate.

To serve unwrap, and cut into 1/4-inch thick pinwheels or disks. Makes 30 to 36.

WALDORF CHICKEN SALAD SANDWICHES

Salad
3 cups cooked chicken, medium diced
3/4 cup walnuts, coarsely chopped
3/4 cup Granny Smith apples, small diced
1/2 cup golden raisins
1/2 cup celery, small diced
2 scallions, finely sliced
Salt (to taste)
Pepper (to taste)

Dressing
1 cup mayonnaise
1/2 cup sour cream
1/4 cup cider vinegar
1 tablespoon honey
6 thin slices whole wheat bread
Butter

Place the salad ingredients in a large bowl, tossing to combine.

In a smaller bowl, whisk the dressing ingredients together. Pour the dressing over the salad and mix well. Season with salt and pepper. Chill about 2 hours.

To assemble the sandwiches, spread the bread with a thin coating of butter.

Spread 2 to 5 tablespoons Waldorf Chicken Salad on each of the 5 slices of bread. Top the sandwiches with the remaining bread. Trim the crusts. Cut each sandwich into 4 pieces.

SANDWICH LOAF

1 loaf unsliced sandwich bread
8 ounces cream cheese
sweet cream or half & half
sliced olives
toasted almonds

Red Filling:

1 small can deviled ham
1 tablespoon mayonnaise
1 pimento, minced

Yellow Filling:

3 hard cooked eggs, mashed
3 tablespoons mayonnaise
1 tablespoon Dijon style mustard
salt and pepper

White Filling:

1/2 (3 ounce) package cream cheese

Green Layer

4 small sweet pickles, minced
6 sprigs parsley or watercress, minced

Cut the loaf into 5 lengthwise slices. Remove crusts. Butter each slice and spread with a filling listed. Place one on top of the other in the form of a whole loaf. Soften 8 ounces cream cheese and add a little sweet cream so it will spread more easily. Cover the outside of the loaf as you would ice a cake. Decorate with sliced olives and toasted almonds. Wrap the loaf in a damp cloth and chill in the refrigerator 3 hours or more. Serve cold, using either full or half slices.

Marilynn's mother, Alice Carlson, served a sandwich loaf for most of her parties and teas, using this recipe.

BILL'S BASIC SCONES WITH OPTIONAL CINNAMON AND OATMEAL

2 cups flour
1 tablespoon baking powder
2 tablespoons sugar
1/2 teaspoon salt
6 tablespoons butter, melted in microwave
1/2 cup half & half (or buttermilk)
1 lightly beaten egg
a little milk and sugar for glaze, if desired

Mix flour, baking powder, sugar and salt. Make a well in the dry ingredients; pour in butter a third at a time, and mix until the mixture resembles a coarse cornmeal. Pour in the half & half (regular milk can be used, but the scones will not be *as* rich). Mix until dough clings together and is a bit sticky. Do not *over mix.* Scones are best when made with a minimum of handling. Shape into a 6 or 8 inch round about 1-1/2 inches thick. Dip a 2 inch cookie cutter into flour, then cut the dough and drop on ungreased cookie sheet, leaving space between each scone. Glaze scones with a little milk and sprinkle with sugar, if desired. Bake at 400° for 18 minutes or until a light, golden brown.

CINNAMON OATMEAL SCONES:

Cinnamon-oatmeal scones are a favorite at Marilynn's teas. Using the basic mix above, add:
1/4 cup uncooked old fashioned rolled oats
1-1/2 teaspoons cinnamon
2 tablespoons half & half

NOT REALLY FROM DEVONSHIRE CREAM

Scones in England are traditionally served with clotted cream from Devonshire. It is not made in America, and if you can find the true imported Devonshire cream it is quite expensive. Use this recipe to make a substitute that is quite acceptable.

1/2 pint heavy whipping cream
1 tablespoon sour cream
3 tablespoons confectioners' sugar

Chill bowl and beaters, then whip ingredients together until stiff. Adjust the amount of sugar and sour cream to your taste. There is no wrong ratio. Cover and refrigerate. It is best if the flavors have at least a few hours to ripen. This will keep in the refrigerator for a few days if tightly covered.

CRUMPETS

3 cups all-purpose flour
1 (1/4 ounce) package active dry yeast
1-1/2 cups warm water (110º)
1/2 teaspoon baking soda
1 teaspoon salt
1 cup milk

In a large bowl combine flour and yeast. Add water and mix well. Cover with plastic wrap and let stand in a warm place for one hour or until batter has doubled in bulk and is puffy. Dissolve baking soda and salt in milk and add to batter. Stir vigorously until well mixed and batter is runny (beating helps to form the holes). Preheat a griddle or heavy skillet over medium heat. Grease very lightly: also grease metal rings and set on griddle to warm up. Pour about 2 tablespoons batter into each ring. Reduce heat to low and cook gently about 7 minutes, or until underside is browned and top is covered with bubbles. Carefully remove rings. Turn and cook crumpets 2 to 3 minutes or just until lightly browned. Grease rings again and repeat with another batch. Cool crumpets completely. To serve, reheat by toasting both sides under a broiler or in toaster. Serve warm with butter and jam. Makes about 25 crumpets.

Crumpets are probably one of the most common English afternoon tea breads. Smooth and golden on one side, the other side is full of little holes through which the butter and jam drip. Due to the rather thin consistency of the batter, crumpets need to be cooked in metal rings. Either poached egg or English muffin rings work fine, but if you don't happen to have such rings, improvise by cutting both the tops and bottoms from 6-1/2 ounce tuna fish cans. Thoroughly wash and lightly grease the rings before heating them on the griddle or in the skillet.

LEMON BREAD (ZESTY TEA BREAD)

6 tablespoons butter or margarine
1 cup sugar
2 eggs
1/2 cup milk
grated rind of 1 lemon
1-1/2 cups flour
1 teaspoon baking powder
1/4 teaspoon salt
1-1/2 cups pecans, finely chopped
1/3 cup sugar
juice of 1 lemon

Cream butter or margarine and 1 cup sugar until fluffy. Add eggs, milk, grated lemon rind and continue beating. Sift flour with baking powder and salt; add to creamed ingredients and stir with a spoon. Add pecans. Spoon batter into greased loaf pan and bake at 350° for 65 minutes. Mix 1/3 cup sugar with lemon juice. Pour over hot, baked lemon bread. Let cool and store in same pan. May be served with cream cheese as bread or tea sandwich. Makes 1 loaf.

When the lemon tree in Marilynn's back yard is bearing fruit, this tea bread is often found on the plates.

LEMON CURD

3 large eggs
1 cup sugar
1/2 cup (1 stick) butter, cut into chunks
1 tablespoon finely grated lemon rind
1/2 cup lemon juice (3 or 4 lemons)

In top of double boiler, with wire whisk, beat eggs until frothy. Stir in sugar until well mixed. Add butter and lemon rind and juice. Set top of double boiler over bottom boiler filled with an inch of simmering water, but do not allow water to touch bottom of top boiler. Cook lemon mixture over medium heat, stirring constantly. until it thickens enough to coat a spoon, 15 to 20 minutes. Pour lemon curd into 2 small jars; cool to room temperature. Cover and refrigerate at least 2 hours. Label and store jars in the refrigerator. Decorate with ribbon bows, if desired. Makes about 1-1/4 cups.

Rich and sweet, this buttery spread is wonderful on breads, biscuits, and muffins or as a cake topping.

SWEDISH SPRITZ

Alice Carlson

2 cups butter
1 cup sugar
4 eggs, well beaten
1 teaspoon orange zest
2 teaspoons almond extract
5 cups sifted all-purpose flour
1/4 teaspoon salt

Cream butter; add sugar and cream until light. Add well

beaten eggs and extract. Sift together flour and salt and add to first mixture. Mix well. Press dough through cookie press onto ungreased cookie sheet and form 0 and S shapes as well as Christmas trees, camels, and angels. Bake in moderate oven at 350° for 8 to 12 minutes. Yields 90 to 100 cookies.

It wasn't Christmas unless Mother made plenty of these delicious cookies. This tradition is carried on by our children.

SWEDISH CROWN JEWEL COOKIES

Eva Rose

1 stick butter
1/4 cup sugar
1 egg yolk
1/2 teaspoon almond extract
1-1/4 cup flour
1/4 teaspoon salt
1 egg white
raspberry preserves

Beat butter and sugar in large bowl. Beat in egg yolk until light and fluffy. Mix in flour and salt and almond extract. Dough will be crumbly. Take a level tablespoon of dough in your hand. Let the warmth or your hand soften the crumbly dough until it can be rolled into a 1 inch ball. Dip the top of each ball in egg white and then in sugar. Place 2 inches apart on lightly greased cookie sheet. Make a deep indentation in the center of each cookie with thumb. Bake in 325° oven for 20 to 25 minutes. Cool 2 minutes on cookie sheets. Remove to wire racks and cool completely. Fill centers with raspberry preserves and sprinkle with powdered sugar if desired. Store between layers of waxed paper in airtight container.

My Swedish friend Eva shared this recipe. The cookies look like jewels, and are good enough to serve to royalty.

TEA PARTY BONNETS

MaryMac's Tea Times

1 cup butter or margarine
2/3 cup granulated sugar
1/2 cup light Karo® syrup
1 tablespoon lemon juice
2 eggs
3-1/2 cups all-purpose flour

Cream butter or margarine, sugar, Karo® syrup, lemon juice and eggs until light and fluffy. Gradually add flour, beating until well blended with each addition. Chill, covered, overnight. Roll 1/3 of the dough at a time to 1/8 inch thickness on lightly floured surface. Cut 30 cookies with a 3 inch scalloped round cookie cutter. Shape remaining dough by teaspoonfuls into balls. Place cookies and balls on ungreased cookie sheets and bake at 350° for 10 minutes. Cool on wire rack. Attach balls to center of round cookies with a small amount of frosting. Tint half the frosting as desired. Thin with enough water to make a glaze. Brush over cookies. Tint remaining frosting. Spoon into pastry bag fitted with a small decorator tip. Decorate cookies to resemble bonnets. Makes 36 to 48.

Decorator's Frosting

1 (16 ounce) box powdered sugar
1/2 teaspoon cream of tartar
3 egg whites
paste food coloring

Combine all ingredients in mixer bowl and beat at low speed until blended. Beat high speed for 7 minutes or until very stiff. Cover with damp cloth.

Yields 2 cups.

M & M® COOKIES

Joan Wester Anderson

1 cup shortening
1 cup firmly packed brown sugar
1/2 cup granulated sugar
2 teaspoons vanilla extract
2 eggs
2-1/4 cups sifted all-purpose flour
1 teaspoon baking soda
1 teaspoon salt
1-1/2 cups M & M® plain candies

Blend shortening and sugars in large bowl. Beat in vanilla and eggs. In second bowl sift remaining dry ingredients together. Add to sugar and egg mixture, blending well. Stir in 1/2 cup of candy. Drop teaspoon sized cookies on ungreased cookie sheet. Decorate tops with remaining candy. Bake at 375° for 10 minutes, or until golden. Cool completely. Good for holidays (where you want some color) or anytime.

From Joan Wester Anderson, whose book Where Angels Walk *was on the* New York Times *best seller list for a year. These have been a favorite of her five children.*

APRICOT PECAN TASSIES

Margaret Sharp

Pastry
2 cups all-purpose flour
1 cup butter or margarine
2 (3 ounce) packages cream cheese

Filling
3/4 cup firmly packed light brown sugar

1 egg, lightly beaten
1 tablespoon butter, softened
1/2 teaspoon vanilla
1/4 teaspoon salt
2/3 cup dried apricot halves, diced (about 4 ounces)
1/3 cup chopped pecans

For pastry, place flour in large bowl. Cut in butter and cream cheese. Continue to mix until dough can be shaped into a ball. Wrap dough in plastic wrap; refrigerate at least 1 hour. Shape dough into 1 inch balls. Press each ball into ungreased miniature (1-3/4 inch) muffin pan cup, covering bottom and side of cup with dough. Preheat oven to 350º.

For filling, combine brown sugar, egg, 1 tablespoon butter, vanilla, and salt in bowl until smooth. Stir in apricots and nuts. Spoon about 1 teaspoon filling into each unbaked pastry shell. Bake 25 minutes or until lightly browned. Cool in pans on wire racks. Remove from pans; store in airtight containers.

FEATHERWEIGHT CHOCOLATE COOKIES

2 egg whites, room temperature
2/3 cup superfine sugar
1 teaspoon vanilla extract
pinch of salt
(6-oz.) package (1 cup) semisweet chocolate pieces
2-1/2 cup chopped walnuts

Preheat oven to 350º. Cover a large baking sheet with foil; set aside. In a medium-size bowl beat egg whites until foamy. Gradually add superfine sugar and beat until stiff peaks form. Mix in vanilla and salt, then fold in chocolate pieces and walnuts. Drop by teaspoonfuls 2 inches apart on baking sheet. Put in oven, then turn off heat and leave cookies in at least 5 hours without opening door (they can be left overnight for convenience). Cookies will be a very light brown color. Store airtight until ready to serve. Makes about 45 cookies.

Regular chocolate cookies have as many as 200 calories apiece. These meringue-based cookies have only 45 calories each.

STAINED GLASS WINDOWS

Marilynn Webber

1 small package chocolate chips
1 egg, beaten
1/2 cup melted butter
1 cup powdered sugar
1/2 cup chopped nuts
1 package colored marshmallows

Melt chocolate chips and butter over hot water. Cool. Add beaten egg, powdered sugar, nuts, and marshmallows. Mix thoroughly. Divide in half and make 2 rolls (12 inches long). Wrap in wax paper and refrigerate. When firm, slice into half inch slices.

These Stained Glass Window cookies look pretty on a plate. They are perfect for Christmas gifts.

SWEDISH PEPPARKAKOR

Alice Carlson

1 1/2 cups sugar
1 stick butter
1/2 cup Crisco®
1 egg
1 level teaspoon soda
1 teaspoon cinnamon
1 teaspoon cloves
1 teaspoon ginger
grated rind of 1 orange
about 2 cups flour

1/2 teaspoon salt

Mix. Chill several hours, but not overnight. Roll thin and cut in shapes. Bake at 350º about 6 minutes.

Marilynn's Swedish mother, Alice Carlson, would make these cookies for Marilynn's teas when she was a little girl. Now Marilynn makes them for her guests.

MUD PIE

Jean Johnson, Everett, WA

Place 18 crushed Oreo® chocolate cookies into an 8 by 10 pan. Mix with 1/4 cup melted butter and freeze. Soften 1 quart coffee ice cream and spread on crust. Freeze. Spread chocolate sauce on ice cream and add chopped walnuts. Freeze.

Chocolate sauce: 12 ounces chocolate chips melted, 1/2 cup melted butter, 1 can evaporated milk.

SWEDISH PARTY CAKES

1 pound butter
1 scant cup sugar
1 egg
3 to 4 cups flour
2 scant teaspoons baking powder
1 teaspoon lemon or almond extract

Remove butter from refrigerator to soften. Cream with sugar until light and fluffy. Beat in egg thoroughly. Add 3 cups of flour and mix well. Add more flour if needed to make a dough that holds its shape, yet is soft. Mix in baking powder and extract. Roll into little balls and flatten. Bake at

350° for 8 to 10 minutes, or until a deep lemon yellow color. Makes approximately 100 small cookies.
Charles Lindberg's favorite recipe

HOLLY COOKIES

Marilynn Webber

Melt in double boiler 4 tablespoons margarine, 30 marshmallows. Add: 1 teaspoon vanilla, 1 teaspoon green food coloring. Mix well and add 3 cups corn flakes. Drop by teaspoon on wax paper. Dot with cinnamon candies.

CHOCOLATE DIPPED STRAWBERRIES

12 large strawberries, washed and dried
tub of chocolate for dipping strawberries (usually found near the strawberries in a supermarket)

Melt chocolate in microwave according directions on tub. Gently holding the hull, dip the strawberries into chocolate until two-thirds of the strawberry is covered. Place strawberries on a wax paper-covered plate and refrigerate until set, about one-half hour.

Chocolate dipped strawberries can be made 24 hours in advance and covered with plastic wrap once the chocolate has set. Leftovers will last at least two days, covered and refrigerated.

HEAVEN'S GATE CHOCOLATE CAKE

Patrice Verhines

1 Duncan Hines© Chocolate Pudding Cake mix
4 eggs
1/2 cup oil
1 cup sour cream
1 cup hot water
6 ounces chocolate chips

Mix the first five ingredients for 4 minutes. Fold in chocolate chips. Bake at 350º in round cake pans for 30 minutes or 9x13 inch cake pan for 45 minutes.

SPECTACULAR CAKE

Sheryl Eugene

1 Duncan Hines® Yellow Cake Mix
1 can Eagle Brand® sweetened condensed milk
(no substitution)

Bake cake in two round pans according to directions. Fill your largest pot with water. Bring to a boil. Place unopened can of Eagle Brand® milk in boiling water. Reduce heat to a gentle boil, and boil for 4-1/2 hours. Turn off heat, and let can stay in the water until it is cool. The next day open the can and stir well. The milk will have turned caramel colored and thickened to just the right consistency for spreading. Ice bottom layer, then put second layer on top and ice the entire cake. For a larger cake, use two cake mixes to make three layers and use two cans of milk. Caution: the cans of milk may explode if not kept covered by water when boiling.

This unusual recipe transforms a cake mix into a unique

desert that will have guests raving. Tell them it takes two days to prepare and they will be really impressed. They will never guess the secret ingredient or how easy it is to prepare.

ANGELIC STAR PASTA SALAD

Darlene Dose

1 cup sugar
2 tablespoons flour
1/2 teaspoon salt
1-3/4 cups pineapple juice
2 eggs, beaten
1 tablespoon lemon juice
3 quarts water
1 tablespoon oil
2 teaspoons salt
1 package star pasta (can be found in most grocery stores.)

Combine sugar, salt and flour. Gradually stir in pineapple juice and eggs. Cook over moderate heat, stirring until thickened. Add lemon juice. Cool to room temperature.

Bring water, salt and oil to a boil. Add pasta to boiling water and cook according to package directions. Drain and rinse with cool water. Combine with the cooked mixture above. Mix lightly but thoroughly. Refrigerate overnight in an airtight container.

Next Day:

3 (11 ounce) cans Mandarin oranges, drained
2 (20 ounce) cans pineapple chunks, drained
1 (20 ounce) can crushed pineapple, drained
1 (12 ounce) carton Cool Whip®
1 cup coconut

Add Mandarin oranges and pineapple to pasta mixture. Mix lightly but thoroughly. Fold in the Cool Whip® and coconut. Refrigerate in an airtight container until thoroughly chilled. This keeps well in the refrigerator for as long as a week. Serves 25.

Yes, serving a salad at tea is very English. This light, unusual salad has been so popular at Marilynn's teas we almost always serve it. It is one of our most requested recipes.

Programs for Teas

Chapter Seven

Anyone for Tea?

A Devotional

Marilynn wrote this devotional to fill the need for a bit of inspiration at any tea. She has given it when she has had a friend or two for tea, at small group teas, and for teas for large groups.

Anyone for tea? Tea is more than lovely, petite sandwiches, scones, and a sweet. It is an occasion of warmth and sociability. It provides the setting to enjoy the company of others, to take pleasure in a friendship, to give encouragement and comfort, to make plans, (and sometimes to gossip, although that would never be true of any of you who are here).

Did you know that more people in the world drink tea than drink coffee? It is the beverage of choice in China, Japan, India, and many of the most populated areas of the world. In England each afternoon things come to a halt as the British enjoy their cup of tea. The experts who watch trends predict that in the United States tea will become the drink of the 21st century.

Jesus often drew lessons from the things around him. Today let's follow his example and discover the inspiration that can be found in our teatime.

(Hold a teapot so the group can see it.) For that perfect "cuppa" the empty pot is first filled with hot water to warm the pot. If this is not done much of the heat of the boiling water used to brew the tea will be dissipated heating the pot rather than to brew the tea, and the tea will lose much of its body and bouquet. The best tea is brewed in a prepared pot.

In a similar way the best results come when God's love is poured into a warm, prepared heart. God is continually showering us with his love to enable us to bring joy and refreshment to those around us. So much is lost if we have allowed our hearts to become cold and indifferent. Instead of glowing, we remain tepid; then what we pour into the lives of others is a weak, watered-down version of what the Lord intends for us to share.

Next, observe that tea takes time.

In her book, *If Teacups Could Talk*, Emilie Barnes writes, "Tea takes time—and that's part of the magic. First you must wait for the water to boil. Next tea takes time to steep. That's a lovely three to five minutes. You can't hurry it without losing something vital. The act of making and drinking tea forces us to slow down—and I truly believe our bodies and spirits are desperate to slow down from the frantic pace our culture sets for us today. People in our society don't like to wait, but you just cannot hurry a good pot of tea."

Tea teaches us to take time. Take time to live. Take time to be quiet. Take time to be still and hear the voice of God.

What tea do you choose? (Take each tea bag from the canister as you describe it.)

Do you choose Earl Grey? Do you see the gray side of everything? What do you say when you wake up in the morning? Is it, "Good morning, God?" Or, anticipating a gray day, do you say, "Good God, it's morning!" Do you expect things to go wrong? As you go about your day do you admire the roses or complain about the thorns?

Or is your choice Constant Comment? Are you always talking but seldom listening? Do you find yourself continually telling other people what to do and how to do it? And how about gossip? Do things that ought to be left unsaid come pouring out?

Or is your choice is Morning Thunder. Are you a grumpy old grouch in the morning? Does it sometimes last into the afternoon...and the evening, too? Are there times your family members know it is best to run for cover?

Tea should steep for only three to five minutes or it becomes bitter. Are there things from the past that you have allowed to continue to brew in your life until your cup is filled with the dregs of bitterness?

Here are some better choices I call Christiani-TEA.

Christmas tea is a Ceylon tea flavored with cloves, cinnamon, and orange peel. It reminds us of the first Christmas when Jesus was born and brought beauty to our lives and salvation to our souls.

Next, there are the wonderful fruit teas. My favorite is peach, but it's nice to alternate with orange, lemon, apple, or apricot. The choice is ours. We can choose our fruit. In our spiritual lives we can choose to cultivate the fruit of the Spirit: love, joy, peace, patience, kindness, goodness, faithfulness, gentleness, self-control.

One advantage of a fruit tea is that it has no caffeine. It will help you sleep at nights. The fruit of the Spirit is even more effective in calming the mind and inviting sleep.

Jasmine tea is a favorite of many because it has the heady fragrance of jasmine. The aroma of its bouquet attracts people. In 2 Corinthians 14-15 we read "Our lives are a fragrance presented by Christ to God. Now wherever we go he uses us to tell others about the Lord and to spread the good news like a sweet perfume." (TLB)

Passion flower tea is a delicate and romantic tea made from maracuya blossoms. In our Christiani-TEA we have a passion for Jesus Christ. The closer we draw to him, the greater becomes the ardor of our love and the depth of our fervent devotion.

English breakfast tea and afternoon tea remind us that we need God's presence all through the day.

What is brewing in your pot is what will come out of the spout. As Jesus said in Matthew 12:34, "For out of the overflow of your heart comes the words you speak."

A tea cozy is very important. It covers the pot and keeps the tea warm and usable. God's grace, mercy, and forgiveness cover us because of his great love for us. He loved us so much that when he saw the bitter tea we often produce in our lives, he sent Jesus Christ to cleanse and forgive us and allow the Holy Spirit to change our lives. Isn't wonderful that every day we can start over with a fresh pot of water and brew some new tea?

Teapots come in all shapes and sizes. A proper pot of tea can be made just as well in an inexpensive, ugly teapot as in a priceless, elegant one. It is not how the container looks, but what is inside that counts. This is especially true of Christians. It doesn't matter what you look like on the outside if you allow the love of God to fill you on the inside. Let us pray with the Psalmist, "Let the beauty of the Lord our God be upon us." Psalm 90:17.

Some say people are a lot like tea—you never know how strong they are until they are in hot water. A Christian, however, learns that faith never shrinks in hot water, but that at those times God changes our old, dead leaves into something beautiful, useful, and refreshing, that brings healing to others. Isn't God great?

Anyone for tea?

Chapter Eight

An Angel Tea

Looking for a unique event that will attract the most people, interest your regular members, and draw those who do not attend? As we have spoken to hundreds of groups of all kinds, we have found that an angel tea has fulfilled this expectation. An angel tea has so many advantages. It appeals to people because they already have an interest in tea and angels. In addition you can have magnificent decorations with little or no cost, use a group activity that will build fellowship, inspire your members, as well as provide correct information about an important, yet often neglected subject—angels!

Publicity

It's so easy to find ways to create interest in an angel tea. Even if your group never publicizes their next meeting, this would be the time to make an exception. Of course you will want to do the usual things. For example a church women's group would make certain it was listed in the Sunday bulletin and the church newsletter. Explore the possibility of having an angel picture along with the article. The church secretary can readily access one from her clip art file. To get attention, instead of the usual flat poster, place an angel figure on a table with a sign giving the information about the angel tea.

Make invitations. First, give each regular attendee an invitation to give to a friend. These should be passed out at the meeting preceding the angel tea. Mail invitations to those on your group's mailing list.

Decorations

Naturally table decorations will be angels. There may be one or more angel collectors in your group who would be delighted to share their collection for this event. Or choose a hostess for each table and give her the assignment of decorating her table with angels. But with the angel theme, the sky is the limit! One group borrowed large Christmas angels from local businesses, draped the room with white cheesecloth material to resemble clouds, and scattered silver stars. Another church had three hundred women turn out for their angel tea. They recognized that would be more than their women's restrooms could handle. Their solution? They took over the men's rooms for the afternoon, covered the urinals with sheets topped with round Styrofoam balls for a head, and added wings. This was one occasion when every woman just had to see the angels in the men's room. Does your church have a banner with angels? If so, display it prominently at your event. If not, why not make one and donate it to the church?

By searching a little, angel napkins can be found for this occasion. Also look for small angels that can be used as favors at each place setting.

Program Folders

Paper stores and copy companies regularly stock 8-1/2 by 11-inch sheets of attractive papers with angel designs. These can be used to make attractive programs for your event. Many designs lend themselves to being folded into thirds with the design showing. Marilynn has spoken to several groups who had members who were crafty. These women made darling program folders that were almost collector's items. Often a church group chooses to include a Bible verse about angels, such as Psalm 91:11.

The Program Itself

There are a number of songs about angels that can be used for group singing. Be sure to choose the ones your group knows. Somewhere in town there must be someone who plays a harp. What can be more fitting? A harpist adds real class to an angel tea.

When Marilynn gives a program on angels she includes many of her unique experiences of how God has used her to be a witness to the Biblical truths about angels. For a very special angel tea, invite Marilynn to be your speaker.

Or feel free to use the materials about angels in this book. "Out of the Ivory Palaces" is an original drama for two readers presenting the Christmas story from the point of view of the angels. Another choice is to adapt the following talk which Marilynn has given hundreds of times.

A Rustle of Angels

A Talk for Tea

Ask the group, "What has wings, a halo and a tail?" The

answer is. a guardian angel being followed by a private eye!

Ask, "How many of you believe in angels?"

Next ask, "How many of you can think of a time when there may have been an angel in you life? Whether you saw one or not, could there have been a time when there was an angel in your life?"

Angels are in! These mystical, magnificent supernatural beings are very much with us. There are probably angels in this room right now. That's not just my idea. That's what the Bible teaches! Yet I have had good Christian people tell me we shouldn't be talking about angels. That's too "new age" they say.

We have good reason to reject the new age ideas about angels. Not all of this interest in angels has been good. In their search for meaning in their lives, too many people turned to the angels, but were not willing to go all the way to the God who created the angels. They wanted a little spirituality. They did not want to go all the way. They wanted the angels to make them feel good. They did not want to make Jesus Christ the Lord of their lives.

To quote *Time* magazine: "The popular authors who render angels into household pets, who invite readers to get in touch with their own inner angel, or summon their own 'angel psychotherapist', or view themselves as angels in training are trafficking in discount spirituality. And churches are at a loss for response"

Time magazine did not exaggerate. Most of the popular books on angels found in secular bookstores teach the very things that *Time* called "discount spirituality." That is the importance of this message. Today we will look at the popular myths that are found in so many of the books, most of the Hollywood movies, and many of the television shows. With so much misinformation about angels, it is not surprising that millions of people do not know the truth about the heavenly hosts. Today we will consider several of these popular myths and compare them with the clear teachings of the Bible. These myths are found in the best selling books in secular bookstores.

1. Myth: When people die they become angels.
   The popular movie, "It's a Wonderful Life" is typical of this view. Remember Clarence, trying to earn his wings as an angel? Books proclaim "We are all angels in the making", but the Biblical truth is that God created all the angels as angels. Angels have never been people. Angels have never been anything but angels. (Psalm 148:5, Colossians 1:16) Disappointed that you won't be an angel? Here's wonderful news that is much more wonderful than the New Age myth. The Biblical truth is that in heaven we will be higher than the angels! Now we are made a little lower than the angels, but when a Christian dies they are welcomed into heaven as a joint heir with Christ. (Psalm 8:5)
2. Myth: People who die become Spirit Guides who can be channeled. But the Bible teaches that trying to contact the dead is forbidden. (Deut. 18:11)
3. Myth: We can summon angels.
   A popular book is called *101 Ways to Attract your Angel.* But the Biblical truth is that angels come only when God sends them. The Bible gives no instructions on how to summon an angel.
4. Myth: We should commune with the angels.
   But the Biblical truth is we should commune with God. The Bible does not give us instructions on how to commune with angels. It does tell us how to commune with God. We call that prayer.
5. Myth: You should name your angel.
   Here is the Biblical truth: Only three angels are named in the Bible. Of the countless millions of angels, God thought it was important for us to know the names of

only three: Michael, Gabriel, and Lucifer who is also called Abaddon or Apollyon.

6. Myth: Angels are waiting for us to tell them what to do. The Biblical truth is that the angels obey only God's commands.
7. Myth: Angels are always loving, never judgmental. Many books teach that angels never punish and are never judgmental. They are utterly compassionate. Their message is, "Don't be afraid. Everything is just fine. There is nothing but love."

But the Bible teaches that there are law and order angels who carry out God's judgments. Examples include the cherubim with the flaming sword stationed at the entrance at the Garden of Eden, the destruction of Sodom and Gomorrah, the death of King Herod, and the warrior angels at the second coming who will defeat Satan.

But the New Agers did not invent angels. God did! You will find God's angels in over 300 places in the Bible. Angels have always been a part of the Christian faith. Let's not let the New Agers hijack the angels. Rather let's spread what the Bible really teaches about the heavenly hosts.

How would you feel if you gave someone a gift that they refused to open? Wouldn't you be disappointed and a bit hurt? I sometimes wonder if that's how God feels. He has given us the wonderful gift of angels to protect us and lead us safely home to Him. But so often we ignore his gift of angels. Instead of daily praising God for His wonderful gift of angels, so many Christians go through life completely indifferent to them.

Recently when I talked to a church, one of the members, Erna Anderson, told me she had heard a pastor teach that angels were only symbolic—that angels did not really exist. In response Erna wrote this wonderful response that she gave to me.

No angels? Would you hush their song?
Call them a myth? A belief that's wrong?
Alas! For shame! No tongue can quell
The message that the angels tell.
To Mary: of the Christ Child's birth;
To shepherds: good will, peace on earth.
To God: their voices sang of glory
As they proclaimed the Christmas story.
To you: tidings of joy they bring.
A multitude of angels sing.
No matter what the world would do,
Thank God, the Scriptures still are true.
So even though the world may try,
The angel's song will never die.

Erna Anderson

The Promises of God

We are here to say yes to the promises of God! Many of the wonderful promises God gives us are concerning His angels. Let me share a few of these promises with you.

1. God created angels to serve us. Hebrews 1:14 "Are not all angels ministering spirits sent to serve those who will inherit salvation?"

2. God's angels surround us. Psalm 34:7 "The angel of the Lord encamps around those who fear him, and delivers them."

3. Angels protect us. Psalm 91:11 "For he will command his angels concerning you, to guard you in all your ways."

4. Each child has an angel. Matthew 18:10 "See that you do not look down on one of these little children. For I tell you that their angels in heaven always see the face of my father in heaven."

5. Angels rejoice when a person becomes a Christian. Luke 15:10 "There is joy in the presence of the angels of

God over one sinner who repents."

Have you noticed? Angels are everywhere you look—in the stores, on TV, in the magazines, everywhere. A recent Gallup poll found that 71% of Americans believe in angels and 76% of teen-agers do. I'm delighted, because it wasn't always that way.

(When Marilynn gives this talk at this point she includes personal information about her interest and experiences with angels found in the opening chapters of this book.)

Let me share some present day stories about the ways God is still using His angels to minister to us.

Guardian Angels

Shirley Halliday was having her regular devotional time. Her husband had died only a short time ago. Her 13-year-old daughter was on vacation with her older brother and his family, visiting the Grand Canyon. Every day Shirley had her quiet time with the Lord. This day her Bible reading was Psalm 91. She read 91:11 "He shall give His angels charge over thee, to keep thee in all thy ways."

Suddenly Shirley had a strange sense of foreboding and began to sob uncontrollably. She felt her daughter Janie was in trouble. Shirley felt helpless. She did not know where her daughter was or what was happening. She began to pray, to plead with God for Janie's safety. She claimed the promise of Psalm 91:11 and asked God to send his angels to protect Janie.

Then Shirley read on in the Psalm. Two verses later she read, "Call upon me and I will answer thee." Shirley took that as confirmation that her prayers had been heard. She felt at peace.

Hundreds of miles away Janie was enjoying the sights at the Grand Canyon. Wanting to get a better photograph of one of the chasms, she stepped over the protective guard rail.

To her horror the ground gave way under her feet and she found herself falling from the edge of the precipice. There was nothing to grab hold of, nothing to break her fall. "O God, help!" she cried.

Suddenly she felt unseen arms under her. Her fall had been stopped and she was caught in unseen arms. But she knew there was no way she would be able to climb back to the top. Miraculously Janie found herself being lifted by those unseen arms. She was carried to the rim of the canyon and her feet were placed firmly on solid rock.

"Janie," her brother cried out. "We saw you fall, and we were sure you would be killed." She was surrounded by other tourists who had seen her fall and were amazed to see her alive.

Later when they returned home, they were showing pictures of their trip. "This is where we almost lost Janie," her brother said.

Shirley questioned what he meant. Janie told her mother how she had fallen into the canyon, and God's angels had rescued her. Shirley's response was different than the children had expected. She asked them to tell just when this had happened—not just the day, but the time of the day. Janie's fall and rescue by the arms of the angels had happened at exactly the moment Shirley had prayed for the angels to protect Janie.

MESSENGERS

In both the Old Testament Hebrew and the New Testament Greek the word *angel* is simply the word for messenger. This is the way we find angels at work most often in the Bible: carrying a message. Angels showed up with messages at crucial moments in the life of Jesus. Gabriel announced to Mary that Jesus is to be born. Angels appeared to Joseph four times, always in a dream.

Four Angels Dressed in Black: Marilynn Webber's Story

God certainly got my attention when the angels gave me a message. I had always wanted to see an angel, especially after reading hundreds of angel stories and accounts. Even when my life was saved by my guardian angel as a teenager, I did not see one. In August of 1993 I had a dream. In my dream I saw four angels, but they were not the angels I wanted to see. They were four angels dressed in black. Even their wings were black. And I could tell they were in mourning.

"Why are you so sad?" I asked. One angel replied, "We are sad because you are dying. Unless something is done, you are going to die."

The dream was so vivid, so powerful it woke me up. Then I woke my husband. "Listen to me," I said to my sleepy spouse. "I need to tell you all the details of my dream before I forget it."

I told him about the four angels dressed in black. "What do you think it means?" Iasked.

"You need to see a doctor," my husband replied firmly.

I had not been to a doctor for years. I had my excuses. My doctor had retired. The next doctor I went to moved to Oregon. I chose another doctor and she joined the army. Before she left she told me it was important for me to see a doctor regularly, and recommended the Loma Linda Clinic. But they told me there was a two-year waiting list. I intended to get another doctor, but the years had come and gone, and I kept putting it off.

After this dream my husband called the Loma Linda Clinic. He insisted that I needed to see a doctor right away. The nurse asked why it was so urgent. Bill told her about my dream. "I'll put you on hold," the nurse said.

Bill thought the next voice he would hear might be the

resident psychiatrist, but in a couple of minutes the nurse was back on the line. "The doctor will see your wife on Wednesday," she said. God had taken care of the two-year waiting list!

The doctor did a biopsy. It showed there was cancer. I believe in prayer and had people all over the country praying for me, including the Crystal Cathedral and Catherine Marshall's Breakthrough. The doctor told my husband I was a high surgical risk, that I would be in intensive care for two days, and in the hospital several days after that.

The surgery was successful, all the cancer was removed, and after a few hours in the recovery room I was taken to the regular nursing floor. Five days later I returned home. God does answer prayer!

The type of cancer I had has no symptoms until it is too late, my doctor told me. If it had not been for the message given to me by four angels dressed in black I would not be alive today.

Angels are God's messengers. God used them to give messages in the Bible. Thank God, he still uses them today. But we must make it clear that the main way God gives his messages today is through the Bible, the teachings of Christ and by the work of the Holy Spirit within us. But there are times that God still uses his angels to give messages today.

In his book *Angels, God's Secret Agents,* Billy Graham wrote that he had never seen an angel. A few years ago Billy Graham was 79 years old. He is suffering from Parkinson's disease and a number of other ailments. Billy has made no secret of the fact that he is eager to lay down the burdens of this life and go to heaven. After a half century of preaching the gospel throughout the world, Billy prayed that God would take him home to heaven.

An angel appeared to him and revealed that his life's work was not yet finished. The angel told him God was not ready to call him home, and that God had more work for him to do.

Billy Graham's associates say that since that encounter with the angel, Billy is working like a new man, eager to do his Lord's bidding.

Hebrews 1:14 states that angels are spirits sent to serve those who are to inherit salvation. That means you and me—today and tomorrow and until we die and the angels take us to heaven.

1. At times they will come with a word of encouragement.
2. They will help you through a time of temptation.
3. They will strengthen you to face the hard times of life.
4. Angels will be your guardians in times of danger.

Remember that

1. the next time you face some kind of unfolding disaster,
2. the next time you make a major decision,
3. the next time you pray for God's intervention.

God's angels will be working on your behalf. They will be there leading, guiding, helping and protecting.

Billy Graham said it so well as he summarized what the Bible teaches:

> "Because angels are so active in a believers life, every true believer in Christ should be encouraged and strengthened! Angels are watching: they mark your path. They superintend the events of your life and protect the interests of the Lord God, always working to promote His plans and to bring about His highest will for you. If we would only realize how close his ministering angels are, what calm assurance we could have in facing the cataclysms of life. While we do not place our faith directly in angels, we should place it in the God who rules

the angels; then we can have peace."

When we get to heaven, I'm certain that we will look back and be surprised at how often the angels helped us and we were not aware of it.

Chapter Nine

A Teddy Bear Tea

Men are from Mars. Women are from Venus.
Teddy bears are from heaven.

What can be more delightful than a teddy bear tea? Grown ups and children alike are intrigued by the idea, but it is the most fun when young and old alike share the experience. When a teddy bear tea is announced, many clubs and church groups have a record turnout. It is especially a natural for mother-daughter events.

Sending invitations is a way to increase the anticipation of the coming event. Stationary stores have a variety of blank cards with teddy bear designs that can easily be adapted into an invitation for your event. Companies that do copying and duplicating can provide you with paper with teddy bear prints you can use to make announcements to send to your members. These can also be used as program covers or posters for bulletin boards. You can make your own invitations using a computer. First try locating a teddy bear design in the create and print section of the greeting card designs. If one is not available, adapt a teddy bear design from the greeting card selections by choosing "personalize this card," then change it to include the information about your tea. Or use a clip art design.

Use creativity in designing publicity for your event. While posters may be overlooked, everyone will notice teddy bears sitting in chairs around a child's table. Just add a sign giving the information about the time and place of the tea. This display can easily be moved from place to place, attracting attention where people gather on different days. One women's group effectively used several of these groupings as a part of the decorations for their gathering. It gave the whimsical impression that the bears were enjoying tea along with the humans!

Make sure people know that bears are not only welcome to attend, but that they will be the guests of honor. Plan some time when the bears will be introduced to the others present. If this is a small tea in your home, everyone can easily share. If it is a large group, make it an activity for each table. Everyone has a teddy bear story. Give the people a chance to tell theirs. Don't expect the bears to take part in this activity. They respect the privacy of their humans too much, and will never tell secrets.

For a group event, announce that there will be prizes awarded to the teddy bears and list the categories. These can include the oldest, the tiniest, the cutest, the most unusual, the best dressed, and the bear that looks like it was the most loved. Make up your own categories. You may need to add additional categories once the guests of honor arrive.

Use Teddy Bears as the Decorations for the Tea

Small teddies make a delightful centerpiece for the table. With a little ingenuity, all kinds of imaginative groupings can be arranged that will be a complete departure from the usual table decorations. A little shopping will reward you with a choice of teddy bear napkins. If you are having a child's tea, you may want to have a separate table set for the bears. If you are having a group, set aside an area in a prominent location (perhaps on the stage) to exhibit the bears that are brought. Put a person who has a flair for display in charge of the arrangement. Plans should be made in advance so that there can be different levels and backgrounds so that all the bears can be seen and attractively arranged. For added interest you can also include a display of related objects with a teddy bear design. These can include teapots, dishes, spoons, spoon holders, afghans and throws, books, etc.

Plan Food that Both Bears and Humans Like

Of course, that would include honey for the tea! Everything tastes better with honey; if you don't believe me, ask your teddy. For any tea, but especially for a child's tea, peanut butter, banana, and honey sandwiches would be nice. Teddy bears are especially fond of bananas, Winnie the Pooh confided to me. There must be cookies, and teddy bear cookie cutters come in various sizes and shapes. You can easily make cookies in the shape of a bear's face by putting two small circles of cookie dough (for ears) at the top of a larger circle, then adding eyes, a nose, and a mouth made with icing. Children enjoy helping to make these cookies; in fact, sharing in the preparation for the tea can be as much fun as the tea itself. Gummy bears add a fun touch.

This is one of Marilynn's most requested talks for Mother-daughter events. It should be given with a sparkle in your eyes and a smile on your face.

Me and My Teddy Bear

A Talk for Teddy Bear Teas

1. How many of you have had a teddy bear in your life?
2. Here is an interesting assignment for the daughters here. Ask your mothers to tell you about their teddy bears. I'm sure there are many interesting stories to be told.

History

In the beginning there were no teddy bears. In fact for centuries there was not a single teddy bear in the world for children to play with and love. It all started in 1902 in the most unlikely place—a little candy store in Brooklyn, New York. The owner of the store, Morris Michton, had recently immigrated to the United States. Morris loved to read the newspaper and tried to learn all he could about his adopted country. Theodore Roosevelt was president of the United States. Morris liked the way everyone called this important man "Teddy."

Mississippi and Louisiana were having a dispute about the border between the two states so they called on the president of the United States to settle the argument and draw the line for them. When President Roosevelt came from Washington, the governor of Mississippi arranged for them to go bear hunting.

Can you believe going bear hunting in Mississippi*?* You could in 1902! Unfortunately the hunting party did not find any bears that day, except for one tiny bear cub. They tied the little bear to a tree so the president could shoot it, but Teddy Roosevelt was angered by this unsportsmanlike idea. He ordered the bear to be released saying, "I draw the line. If I shot that little fellow I couldn't look my own boys in the face again."

Clifford Berryman drew a cartoon for the Washington Post showing Teddy Roosevelt refusing to shoot the bear cub saying, "I draw the line." The cartoon became famous and soon the entire country knew the story. When Morris Michton saw the cartoon he asked his wife to make a small plush bear. He put it in the window of his candy shop next to Berryman's cartoon. He made a sign that said "Teddy's bear". The bear sold quickly, so Mrs. Michton made two more. These also sold as soon as they were put in the store window.

When people kept buying the hand made bears, the candy store owner sent one of the bears to the president of the United States and asked for his permission to call them "Teddy bears." Teddy Roosevelt wrote a letter back in his own handwriting saying he couldn't imagine what good his name would be in the stuffed animal business, but that Mr. Michtom was welcome to use it. The Michtoms realized they had stumbled onto something that was bigger than their little candy store. This led to the founding of the Ideal Toy Company, still in business today. The company has sold millions of Teddy bears.

In 1902 it was not possible to patent a trade name, so soon other companies began marketing stuffed animals called Teddy Bears. In Germany a woman crippled by polio also began making bears. Her name was Margarete Steiff. The Steiff bears first appeared in America in 1903, and they have been famous ever since.

What happened to the original Teddy bear that was sent to President Roosevelt? In 1962 Teddy Roosevelt's great-grandchild was photographed with it; then in 1963 it was put on display in the Smithsonian Institution.

A Famous Riddle

Here is a riddle that was famous in 1908."If Theodore Roosevelt is president of the United States with his clothes on, what is he with his clothes off?" The answer was: "Teddy bare."

Bears of the Rich and Famous

You can find Teddy bears almost everywhere. The rich and poor alike love them. A Teddy bear sits proudly on the window sill of John F. Kennedy's childhood home. Go to Lindon Johnson's ranch, and you will see his Teddy. Elvis Presley's is still at Graceland. The King of Thailand traveled the world in state with his Teddy bear. The late Prince Tulo of Siam had a miniature Teddy bear that he carried with him everywhere. At night the bear went to bed in a matchbox.

One of the most famous Teddy bears belonged to Christopher Robin Milne. Do you remember the name? Winnie the Pooh! He almost created an international incident! Christopher Milne gave the original Pooh Bear to the New York Public Library where he now lives. One of the Members of Parliament in England recently was demanding that Pooh Bear be repatriated to England.

Perhaps the grandest gathering of Teddy bears happened on May 27, 1979 in Longleat, England. 50,000 Teddy bears showed up with 20,000 humans that belonged to them. The average age of the people who attended this gala event was closer to 40 years old than 4 years old. Wouldn't you have liked to be there?

Teddies are big on the Internet. You will find Teddy bear clubs, museums, shops, books, and newsletters. You are invited to chat about your Teddy, and even place his picture on the net for all to admire. The Internet lists teddy bear auctions at Christy's. Years after they were invented, teddy bears remain popular.

Why are Teddy Bears So Popular?

1. Teddy bears are cute and adorable.
   Just look any Teddy in the eye. It doesn't matter if it is

new or old, big or small, or what it costs. Teddys are all undeniably cute and adorable.

2. Teddy bears are tidy.
   A Teddy never throws his socks on the floor. He never leaves dirty dishes in the sink. If he throws a party while you are gone, when you return everything will be cleaned up and put back in place so you would never even guess there had been a party.
3. Teddy Bears make good companions.
   A teddy will go with you anywhere. They are always ready to just sit quietly with you, or take a nap if you are tired. You can take them shopping, or to the movies, or to visit friends. They will go anywhere with you without making a fuss.
4. Teddy bears are friendly.
   When you take your teddy out somewhere, he will smile at everyone he sees. Most of the time, people smile back.
5. Teddy bears are good listeners.
   They will listen to you for hours and hours. They never get bored, even when you tell them your problems for the hundredth time. You can tell your teddy anything, and she won't repeat it—not ever!
6. Teddy bears are forgiving.
   They do not hold grudges. They never complain, even if you forget their birthday, or leave them in the car on a hot day with the windows closed, or go days without speaking to them.
7. Teddy bears love you unconditionally.
   Your teddy loves you just the way you are, even if you are very ordinary. He loves you even when you make mistakes. It makes your teddy very sad when you are naughty, but he loves you still.

What We Can Learn From Our Teddy Bears

1. Be friendly.
   It's up to us to make this world a kinder, happier place. Don't wait for others. Be the first to smile. Do you remember what they call a person who is joyful, warm and outgoing? They say, "He's a real teddy bear!" You can be one, too.
2. Be a good listener.
   This is the best way to make and keep friends. Dr.Paul Tournier writes "You can make more friends in two months by becoming interested in other people and *listening to them* than you can in two years by trying to get other people interested in you." Be like a teddy bear and listen more than you talk. It works. It's harder than you think, but it is really worth the effort.
3. Quit complaining.
   Resist the impulse to nit pick and find fault. I know, many of you are thinking, "I'm not a grouch." But in reality we all complain a lot more than we realize. The biggest temptation is to criticize our family members. We think we are being helpful. They think we are crabby. Most of the time our fault finding does not change a thing.
4. Be positive.
   Let me share a quote from Chuck Swindoll: "The longer I live, the more I realize the impact of attitude on life. Attitude is more important than facts. It is more important than the past, than money, than circumstances, than failures, than successes, than what other people say or do. It is more important than appearance, giftedness or skill. It will make or break a company, a church or a home. The remarkable thing is that we have a choice everyday regarding the attitude we will embrace for that day. We cannot change our

past. We cannot change the fact that people will act in a certain way. We cannot change the inevitable. The only thing we can do is play on the one string we have, and this is our attitude. I am convinced that life is 10% what happens to me and 90% how I react to it. And so it is with you."

5. Don't hold grudges.
   Be forgiving. When you harbor resentment, it hardens your heart. It hurts you more than it hurts the other person. I know how hard it can be to forgive. It does not come easy to me. I have had to ask God's help to be able to forgive some difficult people in my life. My unforgiving spirit did not hurt them, but it did rob me of the joy God wanted me to have.
6. Be loving.
   First Corinthians 13 teaches us that love is the greatest thing in the world. A few verses later it urges us, "Make love your aim." Be sure to keep the main thing the main thing. Strive to always be loving. Think for a moment about your relationships with your family and friends. Would you rather be right…or be loving? Love your family and find ways to show them you care. Love your friends and tell them often. Above all, love God with all your heart.

Let us be thankful for the things in life that bring us joy, including our teddy bears. Let us be thankful for our families and the special love and care we find in our homes. Be like a teddy bear, and bring joy and happiness to those around you.

Chapter Ten

A Joyful Tea

Everyone thinks of a tea as a delightful time. Why not call yours "A Joyful Tea"? Who can resist an invitation to such a happy event? The following is a talk Marilynn has given many times that can be adapted for your group.

How to Become a Joyful Woman Instead of a Grumpy Old Grouch

A Talk for a Tea based on Marilynn's Book "How to Become a Sweet Old Lady Instead of a Grumpy Old Grouch."

How many of you know a joyful woman?

How many of you know a grumpy old grouch?

One of the joys of growing older is that you get to be a grandmother! I have three darling grandchildren, and I've learned to love the questions grandchildren can ask.

A friend told me that one day when she was taking care

of her grandson, the child asked, "Grandmother, how old are you?"

My friend answered, "Grandson, there are some things you don't ask a woman, and her age is one of them."

Later the boy asked, "Grandmother, how much do you weigh?" Again the grandmother explained there are some things you do not ask a woman—especially her weight!

Some time passed, and the boy returned and inquired, "Grandmother, there are two beds in your bedroom. Why don't you and grandfather sleep together?"

The grandmother replied, "There are some things you don't ask a grandmother, and that's one of them. Go see what you can find to play with."

A little while later the boy returned with a smile on his face. "Grandmother," he said proudly, "I've been playing with your purse. I found your driver's license and now I know the answers to all my questions. On your driver's license, under age, it says you are 62 years old, under weight it says you weigh 165 pounds, and under sex, it says you got an F!"

There are some things a lady doesn't tell, but in this talk I am going to tell you how you can become that joyful woman instead of a grumpy old grouch.

As a young minister's wife, I found there were some wonderful people in our church. I was appalled to discover there were also some difficult people as well. Although there were nice people of all ages and problem people were both young and old, I observed that the differences tended to be more pronounced as people grew older. There were some older women that everyone loved to be with. There were others that people tried to avoid.

Morrison and Radtke in their book, *The Joys of Aging,* call them the enjoyers and the endurers. The enjoyers love life; the endurers suffer through it.

When I was speaking in Pennsylvania a woman in the

audience had an epiphany, a sudden insight. She told me that all her adult life she had been an endurer, but now she was going to become an enjoyer.

Dr. Paul Tournier in his book *Learn to Grow Old* writes, "There are wonderful old people, kind, sociable and radiant with peace. Troubles and difficulties seem to make them grow even more serene. They are grateful, even astonished, that things are done for them. They are interested in everything and are prepared to listen to anyone. And then there are awful old people who are selfish, demanding, domineering, bitter. They are always grumbling and criticizing everybody. If you go to see them, they upbraid you for not coming sooner. They misjudge your best intentions, and conversation becomes a bitter conflict."

I do not claim to be a joyful woman. There are parts of me that find it easier to be grumpy and grouchy. But my goal is to make progress each day toward being the person God would have me be. I know he wants me to become a joyful woman rather than a grumpy old grouch. The path I am taking I walk with his help, using the guidance and example of many who have made more progress than I.

Usually when I talk, people immediately think of people they know, both the joyful women and the grumpy old grouches. It's easy to see this in others. But which are you becoming? Are you growing sweeter as the years go by? Or are you well on the way to becoming a grumpy old grouch?

The Good News Is That People Can Change

For ten happy years my husband Bill and I served a church in Springfield, Missouri, the gateway to the Ozarks. A favorite story of the people in Springfield tells about the day a mountain man came to the city for the first time. His curiosity had gotten the best of him, and he came to see if there were really buildings several stories tall.

He walked into the town square and saw it was true. He stood in front of Heers Department Store and marveled at the displays in the windows. When he came to the entrance of the store the door opened before him like magic. What a surprise! No one had told him about automatic doors. He stopped at the cosmetic counter where a woman was getting a cosmetic makeover. "They are painting her up to make her look beautiful," Zeke thought.

Then he noticed a strange thing on the wall. There were doors that opened and closed. Zeke had never seen an elevator and had no idea what it was. He watched with fascination as a wrinkled old lady hobbled into that box. Zeke watched as the doors closed. A minute later the doors opened, and out stepped a beautiful young lady. The mountain man rushed out of the store exclaiming, "I've got to get my wife Millie and put her in that box!" It never occurred to Zeke that there could be wonderful changes in *his* life. His only thought was that his wife needed changing!

I wrote an article for *Guideposts* magazine about a friend who taught me much about becoming a joyful, fulfilled woman. In the back of the magazine they have a feature where they give a sketch of the writers in each issue. In it they included that I talked on "How to Become a Joyful woman Instead of a Grumpy Old Grouch." One woman wrote, "Please send me a copy of your talk, quick! I need to give it to my mother-in-law." That's the wrong idea.

Another person wrote, "I'm a forty-two-year-old witch, but I do want to become a joyful woman. Send your message quick!" That's the right idea. The good news is that even if you are well on your way to becoming a witch, you can change to become a joyful woman.

The First Secret is Accentuate the Positive

A joyful woman admires the roses. A grumpy old grouch

complains about the thorns.

A positive attitude attracts people. When Dewey, my husband's father died, we took him back to Springfield, Missouri, to be buried next to his wife. After the graveside service Bill and I stopped by to visit Helen McLain, a friend we had known when we had lived in Springfield. The past year had been difficult for Helen. Her grown son had died. The husband she had loved so deeply died. We thought it would be a difficult call to make. But Helen greeted us warmly. Instead of complaining bitterly about her losses she said with wonder in her voice, "I can't believe that in the time of your grief you would take time to visit me." As she talked about the husband and son she had recently lost in death, she recounted the many things she had to be thankful about them. She shared her memories with an attitude of gratitude for what she had. Bill and I left feeling blest by our visit and eager to keep in touch.

Almost no one admits to being negative. We become experts at rationalization. We tell ourselves that we are just being realistic—things are bad for us. We excuse our constant complaining by denying that we are a complainer. We're just being honest, we're sharing, we say.

Because it is so easy to become critical, it would be wise for us, on a regular basis, to touch base with a trusted friend or family member and ask, "Am I fun to live with?"

A Thankfulness Journal

One of the greatest helps to me in my Christian life has been this: every day in my journal I list five things for which I am thankful.

It has changed my focus. Instead of concentrating on the problems of life, I go through the day looking for things I am thankful for. Some are big, wonderful things. Others are small, everyday blessings of simple abundance.

Would you like to hear my list from yesterday?

1. my granddaughter, who is in sixth grade, called me on the phone, all on her own
2. A friend gave me oranges from her tree
3. my Lazy-boy recliner
4. the lilies of the valley that have begun to bloom in my garden
5. my husband, my best friend.

The Importance of Attitude

Let me share a quote from Chuck Swindoll:

> "The longer I live, the more I realize the impact of attitude on life. Attitude is more important than facts. It is more important than the past, than money, than circumstances, than failures, than successes, than what other people say or do. It is more important than appearance, giftedness or skill. It will make or break a company, a church, a home. The remarkable thing is we have a choice every day regarding the attitude we will embrace for that day. We cannot change our past. We cannot change the fact that people will act in a certain way. We cannot change the inevitable. The only thing we can do is play on the one string we have, and this is our attitude. I am convinced that life is 10 percent what happens to me and 90 percent how I react to it. And so it is with you."

Practice accentuating the positive. The Bible says it this way in Philippians 4:8-9. "Keep thinking about things that are holy, right, pure, beautiful and good."

The Second Secret Is This: Create Your Own Party

The joyful woman takes the initiative. A grumpy old grouch complains nothing interesting is happening.

I first met Bardy at a church picnic when I was feeling lost. Bill and I had just moved to Seattle after ten wonderful years in Springfield, Missouri. I did feel that God had called my husband to be the senior pastor of the Seattle First Baptist Church. It wasn't our first move, but it certainly was the hardest. For the first time I felt I lacked the energy to start over.

I had been dealt so many losses in a short time. My mother had died. Our two children had left the nest and were thousands of miles away in college. Going to Seattle meant moving a half a continent away from my close friends. I loved the church in Springfield, and during our ten-year ministry there I had developed close ties with several people and felt I really belonged.

There were hundreds of people at the church picnic at Carcreek Park. I was glad for the excellent turnout, but I couldn't help thinking that back in Springfield I would have known everyone. Here I could put only a few names and faces together.

I was relieved when an older woman purposely made her way over to sit and talk with me. She was tall, vivacious, with silver hair and a touch of a Swedish accent. "My name is Gertrude Barderson," she said, "but my friends call me Bardy." She was genuinely interested in what I had to say, and she often laughed as she spoke. Before she left she said, "We'll have to get together for dinner sometime."

"I'd love that," I said sincerely. I remember thinking she would never get around to inviting us.

The next day the phone rang. It was Bardy, setting a date

for dinner the following week. And what a dinner it was! She had gone to the Pike Street Market for fresh salmon. Then she had cooked it with care, and garnished it so it looked like a page from a gourmet magazine. The entire meal was a change from the company meals we had become accustomed to in the Midwest, and it was a delightful introduction to the Pacific Northwest.

As I helped her clear the table, I was surprised to hear myself confiding my losses to her. I caught myself as we reached the kitchen. "I'm sorry," I said. "You have lived here for many years and have so many friends. I don't know if you can understand."

Her eyes were sympathetic. "Oh, Marilynn, I do understand. Even better, I know a secret taught to me by my immigrant mother. You see, she came over from Sweden, away from her family and friends to an arranged marriage. It's fair to say the marriage was not what my mother had hoped. My parents weren't suited for each other. Yet she lived a full and happy life—happy of her own choosing."

"At a low point in my own life, my mother told me her secret," Bardy continued. "My sadness was the opposite of hers. I married a wonderful man. I felt like a schoolgirl each time I saw him coming home from work. He became the superintendent of schools in Carmel, California. Several years after we had moved there, he kissed me good-bye and went to work. I never dreamed that before the day was over I'd become a widow. He died of a heart attack. He was only thirty-three."

After her husband's death, Bardy had become very ill, even wondering if she wanted to go on living. Being a widow with two small sons was not what she had dreamed of.

"It might sound funny at first, but this is what my mother told me: create your own party. Instead of moaning about the bad hand life has dealt you, be thankful for what you do have and share it with those around you. You see, creating happiness for others in turn blesses you. You needn't wait for a special day. For example, today I could have been home alone, but it is so much more fun to reach out and make new friends. There's always fulfilling work to be done, and new friends to make."

Create your own party! What wonderful advice. How it can change your life. It's so simple, and best of all, anyone can do it.

Our British Tea Party

Our family has wonderful memories of the summer we spent in Brighton, England. Bill exchanged pulpits with Jack Hair, a British pastor. He lived in our home and pastored our church in the United States. We lived in their manse in England. Bill preached and prayed, led the church, visited the sick, and had many funerals.

What we treasure the most are the memories of the times we spent in the English homes. We loved the roast beef dinner with Yorkshire pudding in the elegant house of the Habens. Even more we enjoyed going to Mrs. Hardingham's simple flat.

Mrs. Hardingham was a pensioner with a very limited income. Her flat was so small that our family of four could hardly fit into it. But what a wonderful time we had when she created a party! Although she planned a special time for us, she spent very little on the meal.

We didn't know what to expect when she asked us to bring our two children at four, then return for the dinner at six. We discovered the reason when we came to dinner. Mrs. Hardingham had worked in a bakery. She spent the two hours teaching our children how to change a simple, inexpensive meal into a party our family has never forgotten. I recall the meal ended with cupcakes for desert. She had coached our son and daughter, and they had transformed the cupcakes into beautiful butterflies.

While others in similar circumstances stayed at home alone, feeling they were too old or too poor, Mrs. Hardingham opened her heart and her home, and we were all blessed.

Make Life Interesting

Do you catch the idea? Creating your own party means taking the initiative to make your life interesting. Don't wait for others! Abraham Lincoln was right when he said, "A person is about as happy as they decide to be." Decide to have fun and make your life interesting.

The grumpy old grouch complains there is nothing to do. No one invites her to their parties. The woman on her way to becoming a joyful woman creates her own party and invites others to come. She doesn't stop just because her guests may not invite her back. She enjoys the planning and the fun of the party, knowing that it does good things for those who attend, even if they do not return the invitation. After all, why should we let them keep us from having our party? Especially, let's not allow ourselves to become bitter, brooding over their lack of response. Part of the fun can be enticing a Scrooge to enjoy Christmas.

Dorothy Goodwin, who lived in a retirement community, invited her friends to a tea in honor of Emily Dickinson's birthday. It cost Dorothy less than five dollars for the tea, cookies, and napkins. She read a few of Emily Dickinson's short poems, and the rest of the time was conversation over teacups. It was the talk of Mount Rubidoux Manor. There's a million ways to create a party.

Of course, it doesn't have to be a party in the dictionary sense of the word. It can be inviting people to go with you doing what ever you enjoy. It's more fun taking a drive to look at the daffodils when you share the experience with another. In every community there is some where to go that people plan to see sometime, but most people never do. It may be a local landmark, a public garden, or even a new store or shopping center. Are people in your town talking about those fancy new coffees? You may think it's crazy to pay $3.00 for a cup of espresso, but why not try it once and see what it is like? People will love you for saying, "Let's go!" And if the first ones you invite cannot or will not go, keep asking. Create your own party.

It can be a party for one, for me, myself, and I. After all, one is a whole number!

Do you catch the idea? Whoever you are, where ever you may be, you life can be satisfying and enjoyable. To be bored and lonely is a choice. It is not your only choice and it certainly is not your best choice. Life can be fun and rewarding, but often it will only be that way if you take the initiative. Don't while away your days waiting for others to change your circumstances. Create your own party!

Let me share another letter I received. A woman wrote, "After reading your article in Guideposts, I realized that what I need is to get off my pity pot and begin to create my own party. I'm one old grouch that's going to become a joyful woman!"

Isn't that great? Won't you join her?

The Third Secret Is: Wear Out, Don't Rust Out

The joyful woman stays active all her life. The grumpy old grouch sits and rocks.

Too many people stop living. Boredom sets in. Joyful women of any age face each new day with courage and confidence. It is important to have purposeful activity in our lives.

Here I must point out that the mature person is one that has learned to have a healthy balance in life. Nothing makes a person grumpier than being over worked. God has designed us so that we can have a full and meaningful life. Overwork will result in burnout, exhaustion, and collapse. Too little activity will lead to decay. A proper balance produces satisfaction and fulfillment. This is the message I want to convey when I say, "Wear out, don't rust out!" Find that golden mean, the amount of purposeful activity that is right for you.

As you grow older you may have to slow down a little. But don't stop! Let me share a verse from 2 Corinthians 4:16 that has meant a lot to me. "Do not lose heart. Even though our bodies are growing older, our inner nature is being renewed every day." Changes come not only when we grow older, but all through life as well.

That's Why it is Important to Try New Things

Gail Sheehy, in her book, *New Passages*, writes that when the average woman today becomes 55 years old, she still has one third of her life ahead of her. Gail Sheehy tells us that it is important to plan for what she calls the second adulthood.

Dr. Paul Tournier tells us to think of our retirement years as a second career. Like a career, we need to decide what it is we want to do, how to prepare ourselves, and to make an effort to live life to the fullest.

My friend Bardy always wanted to be a nurse. She went back to school and received her R.N. degree at the age of 63. "Then the fun began," she told me. "When I would apply for a job, the personnel director would tell me, 'Mrs. Bardarson, we retire people at your age, not hire them.'"

Bardy told God that if he didn't want her to be sidelined, he would have to help her find her niche. That's when she was hired as a nurse for a retirement home. She was an instant hit with the residents. When they talked to her about their aches and pains, they found a sympathetic ear. After all, she had many of those aches and pains herself!

When her health no longer allowed her to work on the nursing floor because she couldn't lift patients, she tried something new. She began to travel as a nurse with blind tourists. She was paid to see all the places she had wanted to travel to, and she enjoyed describing the sights to people who could not see.

Whatever your Age, It Is Important to Be Willing to Try Something New

A few years ago I took a risk. I decided to try something new and do what I loved. I was an angel collector, but I was frustrated because I couldn't find new angels to collect. I got my seller's license so I could go to the gift shows and find the manufacturers who made an angel or two. I began the first all angel shop and catalog in the country. Little did I know there would be an explosion of interest in angels. My shop has been successful and I have met many interesting people and made new friends.

Next I tried something else new—I wrote a book, *A Rustle of Angels.* It became a best seller. It was translated into Spanish, Norwegian, Korean and Portuguese. It led to my being on hundreds of radio and television shows, and talking everywhere from the Crystal Cathedral to the MGM Grand in Las Vegas. And now I am having the time of my life because I dared to try something new.

What new thing should you be trying in your personal life? In your church?

The word of God comes to each one of us as it is written in Isaiah 43:19: ***"Do not dwell on the past. See, I am doing a new thing!"***

There isn't time in one talk to explore all the secrets of the joyful woman. Let me just list a few that I have developed in my book, *How to Become a Sweet Old Lady Instead of a Grumpy Old Grouch.*

1. Making and keeping new friends
2. You can't win if you are not in the game
3. There are times you should never quit
4. There are times you should know when to quit
5. How to give the gift of encouragement
6. Give the gift of memories
7. The secret of humor
8. The golden key: learning contentment

I have saved the most important secret for the last.

Develop a Vital Faith

My husband asked a woman in the retirement home, "Do you ever think about the here after? She replied with a twinkle in her eye, "It seems that every time I go into the next room I ask myself, what am I here after?"

Two grandchildren came into a room and found their grandmother reading the Bible. "What's she doing?" the younger one asked. The older brother explained, "I think she's cramming for finals!"

A vital faith is more than cramming for finals. It is the most important key to living a mature and fulfilling life. The famous psychoanalyst Carl Gustav Jung reported that in all his practice he had never seen a client come to full maturity and satisfaction in life who did not develop a strong personal faith.

Dr. Tournier writes, "The people who are the happiest and most content are those with a vital faith. It not only helps them face dying but helps them live day by day."

RedBook magazine, a very secular publication, was surprised when they did a large survey of thousands of women. They found that the happiest women were those for whom religion was very important in their lives. Christian women were not surprised. They knew faith and trust in Jesus Christ made a real difference in the quality of their lives.

Developing a vital faith is the most important thing you need to do in your life. Are you making the main thing the main thing? There is nothing in life more important. This should be given our first and best effort each day of our life.

If you find yourself unhappy, the choice is up to you. Our real sin is to be stuck with ourselves and refuse to change. Do you think that God who created the world, the God who created you, is baffled by your problems and is unwilling to help you? Of course not. After I gave this talk to a mother-daughter banquet, one little girl came up to me and said, "When I get old, I want to be just like my grandmother." That's one of the rewards of becoming a joyful, mature woman!

Chapter Eleven

A Tea of Encouragement

Everyone needs encouragement. It may be that your group has just gone through a difficult time. Or you may want to have a tea to give support to those who are often overlooked; the people who are care givers. Even the best organization made up of emotionally healthy, well functioning people would profit from a gathering designed to encourage them. Marilynn has given the following talk to many such groups. Residents of retirement communities have especially appreciated this message. Most often it is requested by civic and church women's groups.

Give the Gift of Encouragement

A Talk for a Tea

How many of you know a person who is constantly complaining?

How many of you know a person who often finds ways to speak an encouraging word?

Which person would you rather be with?

Do you ever ask, "Why am I still here? What do I have to contribute? At my age and with my physical condition, can I do anything that really matters?"

The answer is YES!

You are needed. You have a gift to give that other people need. Some need it a little bit. Others need it a lot. Some who cross your path need it desperately. But everyone needs it. You can give this gift: the gift of encouragement.

Encouragement Has the Power to Change a Person's Life

Dorothy McKinney was content. She had a meaningful job as a practical nurse at Miami's Jackson Memorial Hospital. Although it was demanding at times, she found working with the patients to be rewarding and enjoyed her contacts with the people on the medical staff. She felt she had found her niche. Her co-workers appreciated her as a practical nurse but recognized that she could do more. They encouraged her to go on and take her training to be a registered nurse.

"I was just doing a job, but others saw potential," Dorothy said. After seven years as a practical nurse she began her studies to become a registered nurse. When she graduated her friends continued to encourage her. In time she became supervisor of the orthopedics and neurology sections. She was surprised to receive the 1983 Outstanding Nurse Award and to be interviewed by national magazines. "All this is the result of the encouragement of other people," Dorothy happily points out. How many women have bloomed beautifully where they were planted because of the encouragement of someone in their lives.

Encouragement Can Be a Wife's Greatest Gift to Her Husband

It was a devastating blow to Nate when he lost his job in the custom house. His boss had spoken curtly, "Your services are no longer needed." Nate left the building a broken man, filled with despair. By the time he reached home he was in a deep depression. When he entered his house he blurted out to his wife Sophia, "I lost my job. I am a complete, utter failure." There was a tense silence. Then a smile crept across Sophia's face. "What great news!" she responded. "Now you can write the book you have always wanted to write."

"But I have no job and no prospect of a job," he objected, completely without hope "What will we live on if I struggle to be an author?"

Sophia took her husband by the hand and led him to her kitchen. Opening a drawer she took out a box that was hidden in the back. There was a horde of cash. Nate was overwhelmed. "Where on earth did you get this?" He gasped. "Who does it belong to?"

"It's ours!" Sophia replied. "I always knew you were a man of genius. I knew one day you would become a great writer if only you were given the chance. Every week, out of the money you gave me for housekeeping, I have saved as much as I could so you would have your chance. Now there is enough to last us one whole year."

What a surprise! What encouragement! What a wife! Nathaniel Hawthorn did write that year, and the novel he wrote turned out to be one of the literary masterpieces of the Western Hemisphere. The book was *The Scarlet Letter.*

Do You see Yourself as an Encourager?

Most of us would like to be. I asked a friend if she was an encourager. "I'm a realist," she responded. "but with my family, most of the time I find myself telling them what not to do! I guess I would have to admit I'm more critical than encouraging." So many of us would agree. We may be convinced it's our job to keep our family and the people we know on the straight and narrow. The truth is it is easier to complain and criticize than to encourage, but encouragement pays far greater dividends.

Include Your Family

Be as kind to your family as you are to others. Let them know you believe in them and that they have your support. Notice successes, however small. Be their cheerleader, and like a good cheerleader come to their support even more when the going gets tough. Genuine love results in encouragement.

Compliments and Criticisms: Ten to One

We need to encourage more and criticize less. Too often we think one word of encouragement will balance out one word of criticism. Not so! We are more affected by criticism than praise. We remember the words of censure that others speak and we are sure they mean every word. We tend to forget words of praise or dismiss them as just polite conversation. We believe the harsh criticism but discount it when others say nice things about us. It takes about ten compliments to offset one criticism, Dr. James Dobson observes. With so many critical people in the world, we need to major at being encouragers.

Although almost everyone would agree that encouragement is important, most people have very poor skills in this area. We know how to discourage. No one needs to teach us how to criticize. When encouragement is needed we often do not know where to start and what to say.

Paul Welter, psychologist and author of *How to Help a Friend*, points out that urging is not always the same as encouragement. Urging often creates resistance. A person may feel they are being pushed into making a decision. Another word for repeated urging is nagging. While we may have the best intentions, persistent urging is usually perceived as being negative, while encouragement is always positive. Encouragement shows love. The encourager demonstrates their belief in a person and seeks to inspire them to do their best and feel good about the choice.

Encourage the Dream

Dreams are a part of the process of making decisions, deciding what we should do, and setting goals for our life. Talking with another about our dreams is an important part of developing our vision for the future. The wise adult has learned the art of encouraging dreams. Too often when a person begins to share their dream they are told their ideas are stupid or impossible. Children and young people often find this to be true when they talk about their future. What should you do when someone's dream seems impractical or unrealistic?

Richard Dortch, in his book *Caring Enough to Help the One You Love*, gives a helpful example. Suppose your grandson watches the video of the movie *Raiders of the Lost Ark* and rushes in to tell you he wants to become an archaeologist. What do you say? You could respond, "Being an archaeologist is nothing like you see in the movies. First you have to have a college degree and archaeology is a tough subject. And when you do go to work, it won't be exciting. You may be out in the desert sun digging for months at a time. Maybe you'll never find anything important. Besides, you'll never make any money being an archaeologist. Don't expect your family to support you for the rest of your life!

Why would you want to waste your life that way?"

That kind of response will dash a dream in a million pieces on the kitchen floor. It will rob a child of the exhilaration of having a dream and most likely teach them it is not safe to share their hopes and dreams again.

What response would an encourager give that would still be realistic? "That's interesting, grandson. You've always liked history, and I can see that you would think digging up the past would be exciting. Why don't you save up for a subscription to an archaeology magazine or maybe the *National Geographic?* You can look them over at the library and see if that is a career you would like to have. Maybe on one of our family vacations we could go to a historical dig and see how they do it."

Guidance is given without crushing the excitement of the dream. The grandmother has been realistic but not demeaning or insensitive. The grandson will feel free to talk more about what he would like to do with his life and to share other dreams. He would feel that his grandparent listened to what he had to say, validated his enthusiasm, believed in his abilities, and would be willing to explore possibilities with him.

Encouragers Warms the Soul

My friend husband and I had a wonderful evening as we planned this chapter. We began to recall the people through the years who had encouraged us. My first remembrance was of my grandmother Emma. In my early childhood she called me her little song bird and encouraged me to sing. Together Bill and I remembered family and friends whose words had helped us. We were surprised at how many people there were. We were a little chagrined that we had not remembered more often these good folks whose words and letters had meant so much to us. We were surprised at how many of the encouragers were plain ordinary people who probably had no inkling of how important they had been to us. Our hearts were warmed as we spent the evening hours reminiscing about the people whose encouragement had been so important in our lives. I am certain that each one of you has had more than one person in your life who has given you encouragement.

Here is an assignment. Try it. You will like it. Try it on a day when you are feeling low and you will discover your day will be brightened. Make a list of the people who have encouraged you in your life. Begin by thinking of those who helped you when you were a child. Make a list of those who encouraged you as a teenager. Think of the people who were special to you as a young person, when you were middle aged, and in your more mature years. Just remembering will lift your spirits. You will be helped even more if you buy a notebook and write about these positive experiences. Once you begin other memories will come to mind. You will remember people you have long forgotten and events that once warmed you heart and will lift your spirits now as you recall.

Don't keep this good news to yourself. Share it with others. This is not being vain. You are talking about others, the encouragers in your life. This is a wonderful topic for conversations with your family—something new and positive to talk about on the telephone or in personal visits.

Or try it tonight. When you are at dinner say, "Let's do what the lady who talked to us suggested. Let's remember people from our past who have encouraged us." What fun you will have! You will learn things about people at your table you never knew. It will be positive and interesting.

Do you know where any of the people are who encouraged you? Could you find them if you tried? If you can, why not write them a letter or make a phone call and tell them what their encouragement has meant in your life. You will brighten their day. You will likely receive responses that will brighten your days as well.

Look for volunteers. You will find them everywhere. Often they receive criticism and complaints on a regular basis, but few words of appreciation. When I stop at the hospital information desk to ask directions to a patient's room, I thank the volunteer for spending a part of their day to help me. It's fun to ask them what they would be doing if they were not volunteering. Most of them are busy people who make a real effort to give of themselves to help others.

The people who are paid for their services need encouragement too. You will find the staff will work harder if you discover things they are doing well and compliment them on these things. More improvement is made through encouragement than criticism.

A person who is new to a group or community needs encouragement. They see other people chatting with their friends. Yes, it looks like a friendly place. But too often people are friendly only to their friends and ignore the new person. Remember every new person needs encouragement. Begin with a smile and a cheerful greeting. It could be the start of a beautiful friendship for you.

People need encouragement when life is hard. We often respond well when a person is in the hospital, but if they return home for a long recuperation it is easy forget them. When there is a long illness, the needs of the caregiver are usually overlooked. Cards and flowers are sent to the one who is sick or shut in. The caregiver sometimes is under an even greater strain but is largely forgotten. When I send a card to a shut-in, I like to send a separate note of love and appreciation to the caregiver as well.

Are you complainer or an encourager? Which would you like to be? The choice is up to you. We can all trade grumpiness for joyful living.

Chapter Twelve

Taking the Time to Smell the Roses Tea

What can be more inviting than an invitation to put the busyness of our lives aside for a few hours to share the joys of tea? Most everyone would agree that our days have become too crowded, and that we need to take a break in our schedules to enjoy life.

Use roses to decorate for this event. I spoke to one women's group who carried out the rose theme beautifully. They folded the napkins to look like roses. The plates were garnished with roses made from tomatoes. The napkins and programs were all coordinated for the theme, and fresh bouquets of roses filled the room. Rose petals were strewn throughout the hall and on each table.

The response to Marilynn's talk, which follows in this chapter, has been enthusiastic, with so many telling her that they needed the challenge to slow down and enjoy life.

Taking the Time to Smell the Roses

A Talk for a Tea

I was talking to a hospital group on the importance of taking time to smell the roses. Interrupting my speech, a woman walked to the podium and handed me a note. Everyone sat with bated breath. Was there an emergency, perhaps a code blue and someone was being called out? I took the paper and read the message out loud. It said, "If you don't take time to smell the roses, you may soon be pushing up the daisies." There was a startled silence, then the room broke into applause. The point had been made!

"Confession is good for the soul," the Good Book says. Perhaps my confession at this point may help you to hear and relate to what I have to say. This is the way this talk came into existence.

I was called by the program chairman of a large organization. "Marilynn," she said, "I've just come from our committee meeting. You have spoken to our group several times and the girls were unanimous that you should be the speaker at our big event. We decided you could talk on anything. That's when one of the gals said 'We're all too busy. What we need to hear is 'Take Time to Smell the Roses.'"

"I'm afraid you have the wrong speaker," I replied. "I'm too much of a workaholic. I don't take time to smell the roses myself."

"You should," came the reply. The caller was a strong woman, used to accomplishing her goals. "You need to do this. You have six months to learn what you need to know about the subject, put it into practice, and come and motivate us to do the same."

That conversation changed my life forever. I didn't think I was able to take time off. My book, *A Rustle of Angels,* was a best seller. I was on hundreds of radio and television shows. I had the first all angel store in the country. I was writing another book and magazine articles.

It's been hard for me to change and take time to smell the roses but my life is better for it. I did make that talk, and it has been growing and changing in the years that have followed. It also became chapter 10 in my latest book, ***How to Become a Sweet Old Lady***. I share this because I want you busy women to know I am a fellow pilgrim, as snowed under with work as you are.

But we need to hear:

1. It is important to take time to smell the roses.
2. You need to take time to smell the roses

Even with your busy schedule, you can take time to smell the roses.

Let's Begin with a Brief Bible Study

Genesis Chapter one tells us God created the heavens and the earth. Let me read Genesis 1:31 "God saw all that he had made, and it was very good." So what does God do after the six days of creation? God takes the next day off to take time to smell the roses! It wasn't that the all-powerful God was tired and worn out after His work. Rather He was setting the example for us, that we need to take time to rest. That is what the word Sabbath means. Sabbath means rest.

But, you may say, I'm too busy to take time off. Consider the teaching and example of Jesus. Jesus had sent out the twelve disciples. They came back excited, with glowing reports about what God was doing through them. They could hardly wait to see what Jesus would do next. In Mark 1:31 we read that Jesus said to them, "Come with me by yourselves to a quiet place and get some rest."

The Bible over and over stresses the importance of taking time to rest, taking time to smell the roses. The idea of the

Sabbath is a day of rest.

Here is a story so old that although it is not in the gospels, many biblical scholars believe it to be authentic. The Apostle John was playing with a pet bird. Some of the early Christians reproached him for playing when there was so much work to do for the gospel. John replied, "The bow that is always bent soon ceases to shoot straight."

Most People Are Just too Busy

Few women would argue with this point, but they never stop to realize that in almost every case we can do something about it! Eugenia Price, in her book, *A Woman's Choice*, writes,

"One thing sure, no woman is her balanced best, no woman can think clearly and make wise decisions when she's physically and nervously exhausted. And still woman after woman chastises herself and wonders why her temper doesn't vanish like an April snowflake, when she only needs to slow down! Woman after woman blames her husband or her children when their communication breaks down, and all the time she is perhaps just too exhausted to communicate."

So often our difficulty is that we try to pack more in a day than we are capable of doing. Why do we take on too much? Let's be honest. Often it has more to do with a woman's ego than anything else. If you are competent it's very enticing to say yes, especially when there are those who will tell you how capable you are and heap praises on your pretty head every time you perform. Learning to order one's life is a slow process for most of us. We must learn to say no and take control of our lives. Most of us feel like helpless victims where our work and activity schedules are concerned. We feel like we have no control over many of the things expected of us.

I confess this has been entirely true of me. Over lunch

with one of my favorite people, Joan Wester Anderson, I shared my hectic schedule. At that time it included a deadline for a book, a full schedule of speaking engagements, twenty angel teas to be served in my home in the next few weeks, as well as running my angel shop and catalog business. Joan looked at me wisely and said, "Marilynn, I know what it's like because I have been there myself. I'm speaking from experience when I say you can't keep it up. You have to take back control of your life."

"How did you do it?" I asked.

"I learned to say no," she replied. "My husband made me stand in front of a mirror and practice saying no."

"Really?" I asked incredulously. "You really practiced saying no?"

"Yes," Joan laughed. "It's not as easy as you think. That's why you are in trouble. It's hard to say no. Let me guess. When you do say no, don't you give a reason?"

"Well, yes," I agreed. "Isn't that the best thing to do?"

"Not at all," Joan answered. "Whatever reason you give only opens the door for them to negotiate a yes answer. Let's try it. Suppose I would call and ask to schedule a Christmas tea in your home. What would you say?"

"That's easy," I responded. "I would tell you that all the weekends are taken from now until Christmas."

Joan had a twinkle in her eye as she said, "You've just admitted you don't have every week day committed. I would push for a Tuesday, Wednesday, or Thursday, and you would probably schedule me, wouldn't you?"

"Yes," I admitted.

"There's the problem. You know you have too much to do, but you don't firmly close the door to adding one more event."

"What should I say?" I asked.

"I'm sorry. I'm completely booked for Christmas teas this year. We could choose a date for next year. My first opening is in February. Would you like to set a date for a Valentine tea?" Joan continued, "With an answer like this you have said a firm no. You keep control of your life. You set the alternative that you can live with. But because this does not come naturally for you, you have to practice."

I have been practicing, and I've gotten pretty good at it. Learning to order one's life is a slow process for most of us.

The First Step

The way to begin is by eliminating everything that is possible to eliminate. Your family will probably cheer you on, but your friends and club members may not understand. Your fellow church members will probably be the least accepting. The best approach is to admit to them that you feel guilty about being too busy. Nine times out of ten, they do, too. You will probably be surprised at the support you get if you ask for their understanding and cooperation. Of course, there may be some who do not understand. Some workaholics are convinced that everyone needs to be as busy as they are. The overachievers and perfectionists often think others should be as active as they are. Then, too, other women may have different priorities than you. My friend who is a crafter just can't understand why I don't join her group that makes cute, crafty items. The activity or group that is most important to them may be the least significant to you. If they try to make you feel guilty, don't fall for it. God doesn't want you to be harried and over worked. Don't let someone who likes to play God trap you into feeling a false guilt. Ask yourself, "What difference will it make fifty years from now if I don't..."

So much of what we do, we do so that people will like us. "The girls will never forgive you if you don't accept this job again!" Oh, yes they will. And if they don't, it's a false guilt they are trying to heap on you. Don't fall for it. If you should say no, God will be pleased when you *do* say no and you have nothing to feel guilty about.

Enjoy Yourself!

God wants us not only to take time to smell the roses but also to enjoy the roses—and all the small things of life. Let me read an e-mail that a friend sent:

> "Last week I took my children to a restaurant. My six-year-old son asked if he could say grace. As we bowed our heads he said, "God is great. God is good. And we thank him for our food. And I would thank you more if Mom gets us ice cream for dessert. And liberty and justice for all. Amen."
>
> There was laughter from the nearby tables. Then I heard a woman remark, "That's what's wrong with this country. Kids today don't even know how to pray. Asking God for ice cream Why, I never!"
>
> Hearing this my son burst into tears and asked me, "Did I do it wrong? Is God mad at me?"
>
> As I held him and assured him that he had done a terrific job and God was certainly not mad at him, an elderly gentleman approached the table. He winked at my son and said, "I happen to know that God thought that was a great prayer."
>
> "Really?" my son asked.
>
> "Cross my heart," the man answered. Then he tilted his head in the direction of the woman who had started the whole thing and said in a theatrical whisper, "Too bad she never asks God for ice cream. A little ice cream is good for the soul sometimes."
>
> Naturally I bought my kids ice cream at the end

of the meal. My son stared at his for a moment and then did something I will never forget the rest of my life.

He picked up his ice cream and without a word walked over and placed it in front of the woman. With a big smile he told her, "Here, this is for you. Ice cream is good for the soul sometimes, and my soul is good already."

A little child shall teach them! God is pleased when we take the time to enjoy ice cream—or smell the roses, or enjoy the small pleasures of this world. It is good for the soul!

A chauffeur driven limo roared into the state park. With a squeal of brakes the driver stopped a few feet away from the huge General Grant redwood tree. The window of the limo rolled down and the type A personality CEO in the back seat called to the forest ranger, "Is there anything to see here?"

"Not for you, sir," the ranger replied.

Let these words written by Elizabeth Barrett Browning speak to you:

Earth's crammed with heaven,
And every common bush afire with God,
But only he who sees takes off his shoes—
The rest sit round it and pick blackberries.

But I must admit it is easier for me to work hard than it is to take time to smell the roses. One of the things I have found to be most rewarding is to enjoy the present moment.

Learning to Live in the Present Moment is the Path to Joy

I have learned that life never calms down enough for us to wait until tomorrow to start enjoying life. There is always the phone ringing, the car breaking down, the check that doesn't come in the mail. So what are we going to do about it? Stop procrastinating and start living!

Stop! The trick is to use the daily going-on in daily life as triggers to stop for a very brief moment to move from the routine. These are moments like:

- Waiting for the microwave
- Standing in line
- Sitting at a red light
- Waiting for the commercials on TV to be over.

Instead of being irritated that time is being wasted, stop! Embrace this as a still point in your life.

- Look for something beautiful to enjoy
- Count blessings. Think of what you have to be thankful for
- Lift a prayer—for yourself, a family member or a friend.
- Remember—recall a time that brought you joy or peace, or that made you aware you were loved.

There is a lot of drudgery to most of our days: sheets that need to be changed, dry-cleaning to pick up, garbage to put out. To keep our routine from being all drudgery, Sarah Breathnach advises, "We've got to savor the art of the small: discovering diminutive delights that bring us peace and pleasure."

And we need to take time off each day. The government requires business to give employees breaks in their day. We should be at least as kind to ourselves as the government requires employers to be to their workers.

I relish making a pot of homemade soup for supper. Chopping, paring, and scraping are very calming activities.

I love to look at the colors of the veggies—the orange of carrots, the green of the celery, the pearly white onions. It's a beautiful still life. And what is more wonderful than the fragrance of homemade soup? It makes you glad you can be at your own house for dinner.

Do you catch the idea? We need to embrace every moment. In 1906 Margaret Collier Graham wrote, "People need joy quite as much as clothing. Some of them need it far more."

The book *Simple Abundance* suggests that you make a list of "joyful simplicities", things you enjoy doing—then give priority to doing them.

Such as making a collage for your refrigerator of things you are thankful for. Put up photographs of those you love. Don't forget to include the little things, like the car repair bill that was less than you had feared.

Make your daily life enjoyable. Taking a bath or shower is a necessity. Why not plan to make it a delightful luxury? It costs only a few cents to add a favorite bath oil. It takes only two or three minutes more to luxuriate in the experience of bathing. It is most important to make a change of attitude. Bathing need not be a compulsory chore. With a minimum of planning it can be a time of personal pampering.

Add a Bit of Loveliness to Your Life

If you are like me, it doesn't work to stop in the middle of the afternoon and collapse in a comfortable chair. It makes me feel sleepy, and when break time is over, I find it hard to get up and get going. What works best for me is to plan a time in my afternoon activities where I set aside my work and clear my mind for a few minutes. Instead of doing nothing, I choose to do something that is relaxing and a change of pace When I lived in England I discovered how delightful and refreshing afternoon tea could be. My friend, the author Emilie Barnes, agrees. She writes in her best selling book, ***If Teacups Could Talk***, that the potential of teatime for stress reduction is enormous.

"Tea takes time—and that's part of the magic. You can't hurry it without losing something vital. The act of making and drinking tea forces us to slow down—and I truly believe our bodies and spirits are desperate to slow down from the frantic pace our culture sets for us today. People in our society don't like to wait, but you simply cannot hurry a good pot of tea."

First you must wait until the water is boiling. I like to use my electric teakettle. If I'm just making tea for myself, it doesn't take long to for one cup of water to boil. When my husband joins me or when friends drop by for tea it takes a little longer for the pot to boil. While I'm waiting I set out the teacups and arrange a plate of cookies. Next it takes time for the tea to steep. That's a lovely three to five minutes, no longer or the tea gets bitter. If I'm alone, I carry the tray to my favorite chair and wait in peace, using the time to think or meditate or just relax until the tea reaches its fragrant amber. If I'm with friends, this is a wonderful time to talk.

Emilie Barnes writes, "No, none of these things is absolutely necessary. You can always go back to microwaving water and fishing your cookie directly from the package. You can drink your tea standing up at the counter or gulp it as you run out the door. But again, you'll be missing the opportunity."

It's Your Choice

Perhaps tea isn't your thing. Something else may be. What would be a welcome break in your day?

- Playing the piano
- Working a crossword puzzle
- Writing a letter

- Taking a walk
- An exercise video
- Tending to plants
- Baking bread

Take time to smell the roses and you will be better because of it.

Begin a Hobby

A wonderful quality about a hobby is that no one expects you to be an expert. It's something you do for fun. It doesn't even have to be something you add to life. Your hobby can be something you are already doing. By making it your hobby, what was routine can be fun. It changes your outlook on what may have been a chore. It's fun to talk about it to other people. Here are some ideas to get you started. Could you make a hobby of one of these?

- Sending cards of encouragement
- Baking bread (or some other kind of cooking)

I've taken up a new hobby. I got the idea from a magazine article written by Arnold Bennet in 1924. It was titled, "The Home as a Hobby." I had never thought of it that way. "Your home may be a small one—most people's homes are—but you will never have finished perfecting it," Arnold Bennet tells us.

Today, for instance, I would rather go over Niagara Falls in a barrel than clean out my garage. But I will need some space in that garage if I am going to make some order out of some of the rooms in my house I want to change. Now our house is my hobby. Getting to work on that garage isn't an impossible task. It's going to help me do things with our home I really want to do. This hobby will last me a lifetime. And what can be better than a hobby that lets you enjoy its rewards every day?

Plan a Date Night Each Week

My husband and I also plan a date night each week. It need not be expensive. In the early days of our marriage when money was tight it was sometimes "dinner" at McDonald's, where we lingered over a cup of coffee to chat and share our problems and dreams. We believe having a date night is important, even for couples who have retired. It sets aside a time that is recognized as being special for a relationship. It helps a couple plan to do things together that might never be done otherwise.

Every evening should include some time to smell the roses. Our married daughter, Sharon, believes in using the swing on their front porch. You have to learn to relax, clear your mind of all work and worries, and just rock. Talking with a friend or spouse can also enrich the experience as long as the relaxation rules are kept. "Some day I'll write a book about the art," she chuckles. "I'll call it *Rocking on the Front Porch of Your Life.*"

Don't Live Life Putting Off the Times to Smell the Roses

Circumstances may change. We have no guarantee our health will last, or even that we will be alive tomorrow.

Our friends, Marilynn and Walter Henderson, invited us to join them on a cruise to the Caribbean. It wasn't the best time for us to take off. We had to work at finding the money for the cruise. But we thought we may never have an opportunity to do it in the future. What a grand time we had. We are so glad that instead of making excuses, we did take time to smell the roses.

I visited my friend, Vicki Kvenvick who was home recovering from surgery. When she asked what I was writing, I told her about this talk. Vicki took a framed greeting card off her wall. It had grown discolored through the years, but the message had lost none of its relevance. This is what it said:

> Let me take time to see the flowers
> That grow by the side of the road.
> Let me take time to lend a hand
> That will lighten another's load.
> Let me take time to hear the sounds
> Of happy children at play.
> Let me take time to visit a friend
> Who might be lonely today.
>
> Let me take time to share my thoughts
> With those who are dear to me,
> And let me take time for a quiet hour
> To spend, Lord, alone with thee.

Chapter Thirteen

A Christmas Tea

The Christmas season is a wonderful time for a tea. It is a natural to join angels and Christmas together. Unfortunately many of the programs about angels are not Biblically correct. A common mistake is to make the main character a child who has died and has become an angel. As we wrote the following program portraying the first Christmas from the perspective of the angels we had to use our imaginations because the Scriptures are silent on this subject. We took care to be theologically correct in our portrayal of the angels, basing our tale on what the Bible does teach about the heavenly hosts. Here is the story the way that it might have been on that first Christmas.

Out of the Ivory Palaces

Christmas from the Perspective of the Angels

Introduction: Today's presentation is "Out of the Ivory

Palaces," or "Christmas from the Perspective of the Angels." Our first choice would have been to invite an angel or two to talk with us at our meeting. But although angels are the most helpful beings in creation, it has never been God's will that they appear whenever summoned by humans. So today we have invited two mortals who were willing to come and present a dramatic dialog of what angels might tell us. Let us use our sanctified imaginations and welcome two angels, Ariel and Pax.

(Audience applause. Ariel and Pax come on the platform.)

Pax We are here representing those mystical, magnificent supernatural beings called angels to tell the amazing story of Christmas.

Ariel Some of you look puzzled and surprised. (points) I heard that woman ask, "Is this what angels look like?" Yes…and no. Angels are spirit beings. As spirits they are invisible to the human eye. Actually there are several angels in this auditorium right now, (a wide gesture) but in their form as spirits you can't see them.

Pax Let's clear one thing up right at the beginning. Angels do not look like the chubby little children I see so often in your pictures. Angels are great in power and strength. But there are times that an angel can be more effective if he temporarily takes a form that people can see. This can be whatever form God chooses. In the Bible angels sometimes appeared as a dazzling, bright, holy light. Just ask one of the Roman soldiers who was on guard duty that first Easter morning. Suddenly the predawn darkness was shattered as an angel descended from heaven. The soldiers were blinded as they looked at the angel who was as bright as lightning. The soldiers were petrified and fell to the ground like dead men. They watched in unbelief as the angel rolled away the stone from the tomb like it was weightless.

Ariel Isaiah saw angels with wings, six wings to be exact.

Pax The angels that came to Abraham looked like ordinary men. In fact that is the way angels most often appear. It is possible you have seen an angel and didn't know it. That is why the writer of the Epistle to the Hebrews wrote, "Do not forget to entertain strangers; for thereby some have entertained angels unaware."

Ariel Yes, Pax, that happens more often than most people think. In fact just the other day one of the people here was really rude to a stranger. Lady, do you remember? That stranger was me—you were unaware that stranger was an angel. I'm not going to ask for an apology. Angels aren't like that. We don't hold grudges. But the Almighty doesn't want me to reveal to you the blessing you might have had if only…

Pax (Interrupting) Today we are going to share the Christmas story from a different point of view. This is how the angels experienced it in heaven. We think it is important to share this with you because so many humans have such strange ideas.

Ariel For instance, there is this delightful Christmas story called "The Littlest Angel" about a boy who died and became an angel and his toy box became the star of Bethlehem. How many of you have read the book or saw the story on television? (Encourage show of hands.) What a strange idea of heaven and angels!

Pax People do not become angels when they die. Heaven is not filled with children who remain five years old through all eternity. God makes much better provision for them.

Ariel God created every angel as an angel before the creation of the world. Remember how the Bible reports that at the creation of the world the angels sang together for joy? I'll never forget singing that hymn to creation with millions of angels raising their voices.

Pax What celestial music! The greatest symphonies

and choruses on earth cannot begin to compare with the beauty of that concert. God created angels with the ability to make music that is beautiful far beyond the imagination of mortals. Even you folks who don't like music will be ecstatic when you hear angelic music.

Ariel But let's get back to the first Christmas from the angels' perspective.

Pax Christmas began in the heart of God long before it happened on earth. And from an angel's point of view, that was a mystery to us. You see, God gave the human race a wonderful gift, the gift of choice or free will. God not only provided a beautiful world for humans with provision for all their needs but also gave them the gift of his own presence. If only they had responded with a wholehearted love for God and complete and willing obedience, in time they would have been confirmed in holiness like the holy angels.

Ariel But instead they acted selfishly and willfully. They sinned, and broke the heart of God.

Pax We angels expected God to respond immediately with the judgment they deserved. A holy God cannot tolerate sin. We were poised, waiting for the command to completely annihilate them from the earth. The command never came. "What is going on?" the angels asked each other.

Ariel Angels are far superior to humans in knowledge, intelligence, and wisdom. But we do not know everything. Only God is omniscient. Remember how Jesus taught that even the angels in heaven did not know the time of his second coming? So we were puzzled when we realized that God had another plan for the human race.

Pax (Addressing one of the audience) Yes, lady, angels do sometimes wonder what God is up to. You can read about that in your Bible in First Peter chapter one verse 12.

Ariel Peter was entirely correct when he wrote that we angels longed to look into what was happening in salvation history—how God was working out his sacred plan. Even to this day we angels marvel about the special love God has for you humans. Long ages ago when some of the angels sinned and rebelled against God they were judged. They were cast out of heaven. God's judgment on the fallen angels was final.

Pax What puzzles us is the love God has for the human race. We knew He must have a great plan that would allow a holy God to forgive sin and bring salvation to those on earth. We had no idea of what great cost this would be to God. We did know something was going on. The angels began to ask each other, "Was this the fullness of time for God's plan to come to pass on a minor planet called earth?"

Ariel The Archangel Gabriel had been summoned to the throne room. Although he had been there countless times through the centuries, it had never become routine to the archangel. It was always awesome. No matter where he was, Gabriel was always aware of the presence of God. But when he entered the throne room and came into the manifest presence of God he was filled with holy wonder and awe. The Almighty was seated on the throne. Hovering around him were mighty seraphim, each with six wings. In a great chorus they sang, "Holy, holy, holy is the Lord Almighty!" The glorious singing shook the throne room to its foundation. Then all became still as the celestial beings present listened as God gave a special commission to the archangel.

Pax We have no gossip in heaven. Angels speak only the truth. Even when we discuss earthlings and their sometime sinful ways we speak only the truth in love. But after that meeting in the throne room of the Almighty the news spread so swiftly from angel to angel that soon even the heavenly hosts serving in the furthest reaches of the galaxy had heard and were pondering the news.

Ariel Gabriel had been sent on a special mission to earth. An aging priest, Zechariah by name, was serving God in the Temple, for his order was on duty that week. As was the custom of the priests, he was chosen by lot to burn incense in the Lord's presence. What Zechariah did not understand was that all this had happened by divine providence. Gabriel appeared to the aging priest when he was alone in the temple at the altar of incense. The smoke of the incense rising was a symbol of prayers ascending to heaven. This sincere, pious priest was shocked to see an angel standing next to him, and even more surprised when the angel pronounced that his prayers had been heard, and that he and his wife Elizabeth would have a child. Not just any child, for their son was to be named John, and he would be filled with the Holy Spirit from his birth. Even more startling was the message that this child, John, would prepare the way for the coming of the Lord!

Pax The angels wondered what the message could mean. How was the Lord to come to earth? Whenever angels met, they praised God for His great and wonderful ways, and for the plan about to be revealed to humankind. Then with great intensity they would discuss what this plan might be. This much we knew. The Lord would come in a special way to planet earth. But how?

Ariel My theory was that Christ would come in power and great glory.

Pax But how would that provide redemption for the sins of mankind?

Ariel That was the sixty-four millenia question. My theory was that if people would see the holiness, purity, and majesty of God, it would be a life changing experience. But I could not imagine a way that a righteous God could forgive their sins. So we waited with great expectation to see what God would do next. Of the millions of angels, not one, not even Gabriel, had anticipated what was about to happen.

Pax Six months later the Archangel Gabriel was summoned again to the throne room. This time Gabriel was not sent to the great temple in Jerusalem nor to a priest who had faithfully served God all his life. It was to a young, unknown girl named Mary who lived in the obscure village of Nazareth.

Ariel When Mary saw the angel Gabriel she was frightened. The angels watching were not surprised at her reaction. We angels have learned that fear is usually the first response you humans have when you see an angel.

Pax In the Bible what are the first words an angel says to a human? (Try to get a response from the audience) That's right. It is "Fear not!"

Ariel The message Gabriel had for Mary astounded her. She would be a mother. This good little Jewish girl could hardly believe her ears. Her mother had told her about the birds and the bees and the flowers. She knew where babies came from and this didn't make sense. "But how can I have a baby?" she asked. "I am a virgin."

Pax A good question from a mortal. Gabriel gave her the answer all the angels know. This is one reason we always obey God without question. Gabriel explained, "Nothing is impossible with God."

Ariel Gabriel went on to explain, "The Holy Spirit will come upon you, and the power of the Most High will over shadow you. So the holy one born to you will be called the Son of God."

Pax Then Gabriel waited for Mary's response. The silence seemed to last an eternity to the heavenly hosts that were present as an unseen cloud of witnesses. They remembered how Sarah had laughed centuries before when the angel had told her she was to have a child in her old age. The news Gabriel had just brought to Mary was even more startling; the miracle about to happen to this young virgin was so much more immense. It was even beyond the comprehension of the angels.

Ariel Mary looked up. Her voice was hushed. I remember straining so I would not miss a word. The young maiden said, "I am the servant of the Lord. Whatever his will for me may be, I am willing."

Pax Mary heard nothing, but the courts of heaven rang with spontaneous alleluias!

Ariel Mary was willing. We were witnessing, step by step, God's plan of the ages.

Mary had a hundred unasked questions. We angels had even more.

Pax Now we knew a child was to be born to a virgin. It would be the work of the Holy Spirit. In all eternity such a thing had never been done.

Ariel The angels asked one another, "What kind of child would this be? How can a child be the savior of the world?"

Pax Not even the wisest of the heavenly hosts could conceive that Almighty God, the second person of the trinity, would leave the splendors of heaven to be born as a helpless child on earth.

Ariel Nine months later the summons came from the chief musician. A special angelic choir had been organized, trained, and were told to ready to report at a moment's notice. Pax and I were members of this special chorus.

Pax With great excitement we assembled in the stratosphere directly above the Judean town of Bethlehem. The shepherds in the fields below were unaware of our presence, for angels are spirit beings, unseen by humans. Unseen, that is, until we can best serve the Almighty God by temporarily taking a form that can be seen by the people we are sent to.

Ariel The Chief Musician spoke the word and the heavenly choir took their place in concert formation. The Chief Musician briefly reviewed our instructions, then gave the signal to the angel whom the Almighty had selected to bring his message of good tidings.

Pax Several angels were active in the shepherd's fields

below us. They were to remain unseen. Their assignment was to work with the sheep so that all the shepherds would be kept busy and be wide awake at the time of the angelic appearance. The shepherds were unaware that angels were with them, shaping the circumstances of the night. We smiled as we heard one of the shepherds say, "The sheep have needed more care than usual tonight, but now they all seem to have fallen asleep at the same time." We knew the moment had come.

Ariel The angel of the Lord broke through the atmospheric filament. He had changed from pure spirit to a form that could be seen by the shepherds below. He was beautiful beyond description. His facial features were perfection. His robe was a dazzling white. He was bathed in a pure, radiant light. The glory of the Lord filled the field around the shepherds. They were terrified.

Pax The messenger angel spoke. His voice was deep, clear and melodious, with a power and authority unlike anything the trembling shepherds below had ever heard. "Do not be afraid," the angel said. "I bring you good news of great joy for everyone. The Savior—yes, the Messiah, the Lord—has been born tonight in Bethlehem, the city of David! And this is how you will recognize him: You will find a baby lying in a manger, wrapped snugly in strips of cloth."

Ariel That was our cue. Instantly the thousands of heavenly hosts in our angelic choir became visible to the wondering shepherds below. We lifted our voices and praised God. "Glory to God in the highest," the anthem rang out, "and on earth peace to all who please God." We sang, consumed by our love for God. Our song was to reveal to the wondering mortals below the unfathomable love the Almighty had for them.

Pax It was unlike any sound the shepherds had ever heard. The anthem of praise was glorious, angelic music. It floated upon the still night air. The theme and counterpoint resounded through the sky. It ravished the ears of the shepherds. Never since the foundation of the earth was laid had such heavenly music been heard. We sang with rapture. Then, swelling in a magnificent crescendo, our anthem ended with a glorious finale.

Ariel Then in unison the angelic host returned to heaven, changing instantly into unseen spirit beings. The glory of the Lord, which had filled the fields with an incredible brightness, was gone as well. Now there was only the quiet and darkness of the night sky.

Pax We listened as the shepherds said, "Come. Let's go to Bethlehem! Let's see this wonderful thing that has happened, which the Lord has told us about."

Ariel They ran to the village and found Mary and Joseph. And there was the baby Jesus, lying in the manger. The shepherds rejoiced, and told everyone what they had seen and heard.

Pax And the angels? We saw it so differently. We knew what the shepherds did not know. God Himself had come to earth and had been born as a little child.

Ariel "How can this be?" one wondering angel asked another. "The Lord Jesus, the second person of the trinity, has set aside all the glory of heaven to become a human infant? He came out of the ivory palaces to be born in a stable? He left the incredible beauty of the rainbow throne to be laid in scratchy straw in a manger? The all-powerful king of creation is now a helpless infant? The almighty God who could fling universes into existence by simply speaking a word is now to be totally dependent on a simple young Jewish mother and the village carpenter? How can this be? How can the infinite God now be in human form?"

Pax Heaven was not the same. It was still filled with the glory of God the Father and God the Holy Spirit. But we were lacking the manifest presence of God the Son. We loved him fully and completely. His place on the throne was now vacant, and in a way we could not describe, his presence was no longer with us.

Ariel If there were sorrow in heaven, all the angels would have been overcome by it. If there were tears in heaven, this would have been enough for them to flow in a ceaseless torrent. We missed the Holy One, the King of Glory, the God of Love.

Pax But we knew the Trinity never makes mistakes. Through countless ages we have learned to count on God's plans and purposes as always being just and true, and always for the very best. We could not understand the mystery of the incarnation, but we did know this was an incredibly unselfish act of God showing his infinite love for the world. So we did not weep because Jesus had left us to be born as a child on planet earth, but we did wonder that God could love you so.

Ariel And that is the story of Christmas from the perspective of the angels.

To contact Marilynn Carlson Webber for speaking engagements or books, write or call

Marilynn Carlson Webber
275 Celeste Drive
Riverside, CA 92507
(909) 784-4313
Angellady5@aol.com

Printed in the United States
1023800001B